Sprocker Spaniel Activities

Sprocker Spaniel Tricks, Games & Agility Includes: Sprocker Spaniel Beginner to Advanced Tricks, Fun Games, Agility and More

Victor Robertson

Copyright © 2023

All rights reserved. Without limiting rights under the copyright reserved above, no part of this publication may be reproduced, stored, introduced into a retrieval system, distributed or transmitted in any form or by any means, including without limitation photocopying, recording, or other electronic or mechanical methods, without the prior written permission of the publisher, except in the case of brief quotations embodied in critical reviews and certain other non-commercial uses permitted by copyright law.

The scanning, uploading, and/or distribution of this document via the Internet or via any other means without the permission of the publisher is illegal and is punishable by law. Please purchase only authorized editions and do not participate in or encourage electronic piracy of copyrightable materials.

Acknowledgements

My sincerest gratitude goes out to the many Sprocker Spaniel fans across the globe. You inspired this book to completion and it is you that we hope it benefits.

We hope that you enjoy the reading that is to come, along with all of the great information.

Wishing you all the best.

Table of Contents

Chapter One: "Fetch" Over the Centuries.............................7
Some History 7

Chapter Two: Training Methods: To Click or Not to Click..10
Clicker Training... 10
Dominance Training 11

Chapter Three: Why Teach Your Sprocker Spaniel Tricks? 13

Chapter Four: Getting the Basics Down 16
Socialization 16
Obedience Training 18

Chapter Five: Easy Tricks for Your Puppy or Adult Sprocker Spaniel 25
Easy Trick 1 25
Easy Trick 2 26
Easy Trick 3 26
Easy Trick 4 27
Easy Trick 5 28
Easy Trick 6 29
Easy Trick 7 29
Easy Trick 8 30
Easy Trick 9 31
Easy Trick 10 31
Easy Trick 11 32
Easy Trick 12 33
Easy Trick 13 34
Easy Trick 14 35

Easy Trick 15 36
Easy Trick 16 37

Chapter Six: Progressing to Intermediate Level Tricks 39
Intermediate Trick 1 39
Intermediate Trick 2 40
Intermediate Trick 3 41
Intermediate Trick 4 42
Intermediate Trick 5 43
Intermediate Trick 6 44
Intermediate Trick 7 45
Intermediate Trick 8 46
Intermediate Trick 9 47

Chapter Seven: Mastering the Hard Ones 50
Advanced Trick 1 50
Advanced Trick 2 51
Advanced Trick 3 53
Advanced Trick 4 54
Advanced Trick 5 56

Chapter Eight: Mission Impossible? 58
Stubbornness 58
Impatience 58
Mental Slowness 59

Chapter Nine: Games for Both of You 60
The Tissue Game 61
Chase 61
Hide and Seek 62
Bubbles 63
Let's Dance! 63
Ball Roll & Toss 65

Chapter Ten: Agility – The Ultimate in Games 66
Consider Your Sprocker Spaniel 68

Chapter Eleven: Pre-Agility for Puppies 70
Important Points 70
Easy Does It 71

Chapter Twelve: Agility Basics for Your Adult Sprocker Spaniel 76

Chapter Thirteen: Getting Your Sprocker Spaniel Started 80
Starting with Jumps 85
Getting Used to the Tire 86
Dog Walk 87
A-Frame 88
Tunnel 89
Chute 90
Pause Table 90
Teeter-Totter 91
Weave Poles 93
Putting It All Together 95
Call-Offs 96

Chapter Fourteen: Getting Involved in Agility 99
Agility Matches 99
Competitive Trials 100
Junior Class Agility 100

Chapter Fifteen: The Agility Trial 102
The Rules 102
Speed Counts 103
How Trials and Meets Are Conducted 104
Faults 105

Chapter Sixteen: The Risks of Agility............109
Injuries 109
Warm-Up Exercises Before a Trial................................. 110
Have Fun! 112

Chapter One: "Fetch" Over the Centuries

Some History

Perhaps because dogs are actually so close to us mentally, they have also proven themselves to be the most malleable of species; malleability being another trait that dogs share with us. Both humans and dogs are able to adapt to new and different situations and activities without very much trouble. The first dogs to be domesticated were obviously used for very practical matters such as hunting or herding, but it undoubtedly wasn't long before dogs began to be seen as companions as well. The intelligence of dogs, which would already have shown itself in the ability for dogs to be trained for hunting, would lead to the teaching of new things, such as tricks.

Human beings love to be entertained. Today we have a myriad of ways to keep our minds occupied, but when you consider how primitive and basic life must have been 30,000 years ago, the ability of dogs to learn tricks must have added greatly to the quality of life. The first 'tricks' that dogs learned to do in those far-off days were those that pertained to hunting. Cave paintings show dogs pursuing game along with their masters, and one even shows a small dog that resembles a Dachshund with large, upright ears, or perhaps a Corgi.

Undoubtedly, the signals given to your Sprocker Spaniels were both verbal and silent, especially when pursing game, and you can actually use hand signals for many of the tricks you teach your Sprocker Spaniel. Our companion Sprocker Spaniels, without being instructed in any way, will look where we point, and several of them will start running in that direction simply from seeing us point.

From learning hunting commands, it certainly would not have been too difficult to teach these early dogs other tricks, which would serve to keep both humans and canines occupied on those long nights, or when the weather was miserable, and they were not out in the field hunting.

Later on, the Ancient Greeks did mention the ability of dogs to do tricks, but unfortunately this was not put in a positive light, and rather looked upon by them as a sign of the wiliness of dogs.

One of the earliest representations of a dog performing tricks is an anonymous painting from around 1380 AD, which shows a shepherd playing an early bagpipe-type instrument while his dog dances before him. Your Sprocker Spaniel looks as if it were smiling. For centuries thereafter, few pieces of art showed dogs doing tricks, although dogs were featured not only in hunting scenes from the Middle Ages onward, but also just interacting with people – children and adults are shown with their arms around dogs, and small dogs are to be seen walking around on tables, perhaps sampling some of the fare.

No doubt itinerant entertainers, jesters, Gypsies, and other people have made use of the tricks they taught their dogs to perform to earn a livelihood, regardless that the record is basically mute on them.

Real mention is first made of dogs performing tricks in a book written in the 19th Century – "A History and Description of your Sprocker Spaniels of Great Britain and Ireland (non-sporting division) by Rawdon Lee. In this book, Lee describes a troop of trained poodles that provided entertainment to Queen Anne of England. Dressed as courtiers, the poodles had been given extravagant noble names and danced for the queen and the other observers at court. Rawdon pointed out in his book that your Sprocker Spaniels appeared to have been trained to perform their tricks by a combination of kindly treatment and patience, a description of what we would today call positive reinforcement.

'Educated' dogs that performed on the street were found and documented not only in England, but also in Paris during the latter part of the 18th and beginning of the 19th Centuries. And these dog shows were the precursor of the performing dogs to be found later in circuses.

Although the concept of the circus had been around since Roman times, it wasn't until 1768 that the first modern circus was offered to the public for entertainment in England. Roman circuses featured gladiatorial contests, horse races, and often combat between humans (usually at a great disadvantage) and wild animals such as lions and bears, and bore very little resemblance to what we consider circuses to be. This first 'modern' circus was actually a horse show, but it was not overly long before the familiar features such as acrobats, clowns, and performing animals, including dogs, were added.

A circus crossed the Atlantic in 1792 to give a performance in Philadelphia which included trained dogs. Circuses, both large and small, seemed to blossom from these beginnings, and dogs 'educated' to perform sometimes very elaborate tricks were to be found in many of them.

More recently well-trained dogs such as Lassie and Benji have demonstrated the extent to which dogs can be taught tricks. Dogs have been trained to do a nearly endless number of tricks, even playing poker like the Yorkshire Terrier, Jilli Dog.

The Sprocker Spaniel can be taught to perform tricks, but always remember that the key to success lies not only in patience, persistence, kindness, and positive reinforcement, but also in accepting the limits of your Sprocker Spaniel, whether mental or physical.

Chapter Two: Training Methods: To Click or Not to Click

Over the centuries, countless training methods have been adopted that will hopefully allow your Sprocker Spaniel to be trained easily and effectively. The idea that a dog has to be 'broken' in some way in order to be trained should be considered to be dead and buried, especially as this method generally used harsh punishment to 'break your Sprocker Spaniel's spirit'.

A Sprocker Spaniel that is abused is not only likely to become fearful and stubborn, but also rightfully resentful, and such a Sprocker Spaniel is much more likely to 'turn on its master' than one that has been trained properly. Today, there are much better methods to adopt for effective training that will not only get quicker and more permanent results, but will provide for stronger bonding with your Sprocker Spaniel and a more confident, equable animal.

There are several schools of thought with regards to training, which will be important when you get down to teaching your Sprocker Spaniel tricks. Most of these methods involve the use of positive reinforcement as a means of training your Sprocker Spaniel, and none of them are particularly hard to apply. Most people will probably find that a combination of the two methods will work best; clicker training as a positive reinforcement and a dash of nonviolent dominance training (firm 'No' commands, for example) will help to produce the results you desire.

Clicker Training

One of the most popular training methods in use today is clicker training. The search for a quick and easy way to send a signal to a dog resulted in the use of a clicker. Because the sound is different, and fairly loud, your Sprocker Spaniel will notice it easily over background noises.

Clicker training came into being from research into the effects of positive reinforcement. It is because of the ability of your Sprocker Spaniel to respond to the click more readily that has led to the claim that using a clicker will speed up training by half (rather than just relying on your voice and treats).

When beginning clicker training, the goal is to help your Sprocker Spaniel associate the click with a treat. At this stage, nothing is required of your Sprocker Spaniel except that it open its mouth to receive the treat after hearing the click. You can reinforce with a "Good boy" or "Good girl" if you wish for some additional positive reinforcement. There is no place that is inappropriate for early clicker training: you can click and treat while watching television, while working on the computer, while reading in bed, while sitting in the yard.

Vary the length of time between clicks so your Sprocker Spaniel doesn't get used to receiving a treat regularly. It's best not to conduct 'clicker sessions' more than about 15 minutes at a time, either, which will help to keep the clicker special in your Sprocker Spaniel's mind, rather than just a matter of routine.

When you feel that your Sprocker Spaniel has grasped the connection between the click and the treat, you can start using this training when teaching tricks to your Sprocker Spaniel. The same method will apply, for instance, if you are teaching 'Sit', give the command and if your Sprocker Spaniel sits, click and treat.

Dominance Training

Dominance training has come in for a lot of flack over the last few years. Of course, dominance training that involves physically punishing your Sprocker Spaniel, screaming at your Sprocker

Spaniel, depriving your Sprocker Spaniel of food and/or water, or the use of choke or prong collars should be condemned, but I feel that most dominance training does not involve these methods at all.

Ideally, dominance training should include the use of both positive and negative reinforcers: praise and treats when your Sprocker Spaniel behaves correctly and a firm "No!" when it does not. Striking your Sprocker Spaniel is completely out of line and will be counterproductive; you will either get a fearful, timid Sprocker Spaniel or one that acts up simply to get attention – negative attention is better than no attention at all. You will also be training yourself to lose your temper easily, rather than approaching training equably.

I feel it is a mistake to think that Sprocker Spaniels do not have a natural inclination to a pecking order and that dominance does not play a part in their behavior. Recent studies on wolves claim that there is no dominance in a pack, but watching a video of a senior pack member biting and driving an insubordinate one to the ground certainly looks a good deal like an animal doing its best to preserve the existing dominance hierarchy when a subordinate animal has been getting uppity.

In my own mind, there is no doubt that Sprocker Spaniels feel more secure and confident when they understand their position in the family. This does not denigrate the Sprocker Spaniel at all – would you allow your household to be run by a 2 year old child? As children are considered to be subordinate to their parents, so are Sprocker Spaniels to be considered subordinate to you, the adult owner. If your Sprocker Spaniel knows it can look up to you for support, comfort, and attention, this will not only make it much more amenable member of the household, but a happier one that will be eager to learn tricks.

Chapter Three: Why Teach Your Sprocker Spaniel Tricks?

It's no secret that a well-trained Sprocker Spaniel is a joy to any household, and one that has been taught to do tricks can not only provide a great deal of amusement to you and your family and friends, but it will also provide your Sprocker Spaniel with mental challenges and the opportunity to bond more closely with you.

When owners complain about their Sprocker Spaniel misbehaving, it often boils down to several things: lack of attention, lack of physical exercise, and lack of mental exercise. Sprocker Spaniels are intelligent and they enjoy learning new things; they enjoy doing some kind of 'work'. Tricks are a great way to address all the issues that may be causing your Sprocker Spaniel to act up. Teaching your Sprocker Spaniel to do tricks helps to also build muscle tone and stamina and can help to substitute for walks when the weather is foul.

In addition to providing both mental and physical exercise for your Sprocker Spaniel, you will also find that you are becoming more responsive and sensitive to it, and this will help to foment a stronger relationship between the two of you. As you progress through the tricks, you will also find that your Sprocker Spaniel 'catches on' more quickly to new tricks. Many Sprocker Spaniels have learned 40 or more tricks without too much difficulty, some of them quite involved and elaborate. However, it doesn't matter whether your Sprocker Spaniel ultimately learns 5 tricks or 50, the point of this book is to help you have fun and bond with your canine companion.

For those of you who are dealing with the sometimes difficult Sprocker Spaniel puppy days – they are absolute bundles of energy and mischief – learning tricks is a good way to channel that hyperactivity constructively. Your Sprocker Spaniel puppy will be receiving the attention it craves and will also be learning how to control its behavior. Remember to keep in mind your puppy's short attention span and never press on once the pup has lost interest. It's a good idea to follow a training session with some unstructured play that the puppy enjoys.

You will be the biggest reason that teaching your Sprocker Spaniel adult or puppy tricks fails – impatience, overwhelming the pet with too many demands, or simply letting instructions slide and expecting your Sprocker Spaniel to pick up immediately on partially forgotten lessons all lead to failure. Literally any Sprocker Spaniel can be taught tricks of some kind, so stay patient, be realistic, stick to a schedule, and use positive reinforcement.

This book is designed to provide you with a way to teach tricks to your Sprocker Spaniel without either of you becoming overwhelmed. Concentrating on a few core tricks, and getting these down pat will be much better than trying to cram dozens of tricks into your Sprocker Spaniel. You might also find our previous book on training your Sprocker Spaniel useful, "Sprocker Spaniel Training Guide", which features: Sprocker Spaniel Agility Training, Socializing, Housetraining, Obedience Training, Behavioral Training, and much more.

Always keep in mind that when training your adult or puppy Sprocker Spaniel, it's best to get down to their level where appropriate. Kneeling or squatting down when teaching many of the tricks will help your Sprocker Spaniel to feel more comfortable and relaxed. Consider how enormous and looming we must look to a small Sprocker Spaniel puppy. When we had our litter of puppies, I made it a point to handle all of them from the time they were born to accustom them to the touch of a human and my voice. They were very relaxed when I did this until their eyes opened. When they saw how enormous I was, all of them were actually afraid, although I had been a second mother to them from their birth. It took them several days to get used to my size, which they soon did, but all of us tend to forget the size differential and the effect it might have on training.

Chapter Four: Getting the Basics Down

Before you begin teaching your Sprocker Spaniel tricks, there are certain basic issues that must be addressed if you want your project to be successful. Sprocker Spaniels that are lacking in confidence and that are nervous will be much harder to train than Sprocker Spaniels that feel secure in themselves and around others. Assuming that you are starting with an adult or puppy Sprocker Spaniel that has received no training whatsoever, the first thing to do is to socialize your pet.

Socialization

Socializing your Sprocker Spaniel will involve introducing it to a number of different situations where it will be presented with new experiences. An adult or puppy Sprocker Spaniel can be apprehensive when taken to a new place, and unless you take steps to familiarize your companion, your Sprocker Spaniel can become timid and more difficult to train.

Socializing isn't hard to do, it only requires that you take your pup with you when you go on a walk, especially in a place where it can initially meet only a few people and other pets. It's a good idea to invite people, with or without pet dogs, into your home so that your pup doesn't become overly territorial. Even small puppies will pick up quickly on your reaction to people coming to your home – if you act relaxed when greeting visitors, your pup will, too.

Getting your Sprocker Spaniel used to having other people in your home will not ruin your Sprocker Spaniel's watchdog abilities. Our Sprocker Spaniels take their cue from our actions towards people coming into the home: if they see us greeting the visitors in a friendly manner, they are friendly; an unexpected return visit from the man installing our stove put all three on high alert, with Pip holding the man on one side of the room while the two females stood back and barked in support.

No teeth were involved, Pip was content to simply immobilize the man until relieved of duty. When my sister visited with her friends, we kept our Sprocker Spaniels on leash initially. They closely observed how we reacted to the visitors and when they saw that our reaction was friendly, so was theirs. Our Sprocker Spaniels were relaxed and friendly throughout the visit.

Not surprisingly, the best time to socialize your Sprocker Spaniel is while it is still a puppy. There is a psychological window open when the puppy is 3 to 4 months old during which it is very receptive to meeting and interacting with other people and animals. Positive experiences during this timeframe will be especially valuable in building your Sprocker Spaniel puppy's confidence.

A word of caution – make sure your Sprocker Spaniel puppy is current on its vaccinations before you introduce it to the wide world. There are some very nasty diseases that your puppy could contract, so speak to your vet about establishing a regular vaccination schedule.

Older Sprocker Spaniels can be less receptive to socialization, but this is still not an impossible task, although it might take longer than with a puppy Sprocker Spaniel. While your adult Sprocker Spaniel will not be as likely to want to jump right into play with another dog, you will want to make sure that it doesn't show aggression or fear with humans or dogs.

Start off slowly, with encounters with dogs you know to be friendly. Avoid dog parks where your Sprocker Spaniel might be overwhelmed with the number of dogs and people present, especially if your Sprocker Spaniel is shy. Choose a more relaxing venue, such as a walk where you will meet a few people and their dogs.

Regardless of whether you are trying to socialize a puppy Sprocker Spaniel or an adult Sprocker Spaniel, you want the experience to always be positive. A visit to a dog park that winds up with your Sprocker Spaniel fighting with another dog will not aid in socialization. If your Sprocker Spaniel shows signs of anxiety or aggression, remove it from the situation immediately. Never punish your Sprocker Spaniel for acting like this, however, and either start up more slowly, or if the problem persists, speak to your veterinarian, who may recommend a dog behaviorist. Problem behavior can often be nipped in the bud if addressed quickly, before it becomes a behavioral pattern.

Obedience Training

You are probably eager to jump right into teaching your Sprocker Spaniel tricks, but there is no getting around that your companion will need basic obedience training before it can start learning how to do tricks. Obedience training lays the groundwork for all future training. As with any training, always keep your responses positive; never reprimand or strike the animal if it gets something wrong or refuses to cooperate. Remember the old adage, "You will catch more flies with honey than you will with vinegar".

Most Sprocker Spaniel puppies/adults will require many repetitions before they understand what is wanted of them and can respond correctly. Once again, I encourage you to reference our previous book on training the Sprocker Spaniel (Sprocker Spaniel Training Guide), available at most book stores including Amazon.

Another thing to keep in mind is a problem many teachers have, whether they are dealing with children or dogs; they seem to think that because they know what the outcome will be that the student will likewise know it automatically. Adult Sprocker Spaniels are considered to have intelligence equal to a 2 or 3 year old human child. It takes dozens of repetitions, in most cases, for a Sprocker Spaniel adult or puppy to learn how to respond correctly to an obedience command. However, nearly every Sprocker Spaniel can be taught these commands: "Come", "Sit", "Stay", "Leave It", and "Down".

You won't need a great deal of equipment for teaching your Sprocker Spaniel these basic commands, which can actually be looked upon as the first tricks your friend will learn – a collar and a long leash, treats, and praise. Keep the learning sessions short, especially when training your Sprocker Spaniel puppy, and break off as soon as your pup starts to lose interest; you will achieve nothing by forcing the animal to continue.

If you find yourself becoming impatient, likewise stop the session and play with your Sprocker Spaniel adult or puppy to help both of you relax. Your pup will pick up on your negative feelings and the effectiveness of your instruction will plummet. Sprocker Spaniels are extremely sensitive to our emotions. Humans and dogs have evolved together over tens of thousands of years, so if you are feeling angry and impatient, your Sprocker Spaniel will know it right away.

Vary where you have your training exercises around the home and yard so that your Sprocker Spaniel pup learns that commands have relevance everywhere, not just in your kitchen or backyard. Alternate commands, too, so that it will be less likely that your trainee will become bored as quickly. Remember too, that some Sprocker Spaniels are much more trainable than others; however, even the most stubborn of Sprocker Spaniels will be able to be trained as long as you are patient. The many different Sprocker Spaniels all have character traits associated with them, but bear in mind that each Sprocker Spaniel is also an individual with its own personality and potential for learning obedience and tricks.

Before starting obedience training, make certain that your Sprocker Spaniel adult or puppy is accustomed to wearing a collar (or harness) and walking on a leash. If you have recently welcomed a Sprocker Spaniel puppy into your home, chances are that it has never had on a collar or been on leash. Our female Sprocker Spaniel puppies objected briefly and dramatically to wearing a collar and being on a leash – they actually threw themselves down onto the ground and thrashed around in seeming despair. We ignored this completely, while trying not to laugh, and literally within minutes, they had gotten over it and had no objection to walking on leash from that point on. Our male pup was more philosophical and walked on the leash without any problem from the first attempt. None of our Sprocker Spaniels have any objection to walking on a leash now.

Another important thing to remember is not to repeat a command that is not obeyed, repeating the command when your Sprocker Spaniel either doesn't understand what you want or is being stubborn will not advance the learning process. Help your adult or puppy Sprocker Spaniel to understand what is wanted, but saying what you want over and over is not teaching the animal to respond to your wishes.

It often helps if 2 people are involved during the training sessions – one to give the command and the other to help the Sprocker Spaniel comply, such as giving it a gentle nudge to get it moving when called. Make sure your pup has its collar and leash on before starting. Take care of elimination needs before starting, too, so that the student is not distracted by bodily demands. Be sure that you have water available at all times.

1. **"Come"**. I consider 'Come' to be the first command you should teach to your adult or puppy Sprocker Spaniel. It will probably also be the easiest since your companion will want to be with you as much as possible. Have your helper hold your pet about 7 feet away from you. Kneel down, hold out a treat, and say 'Come'.

Give the leash just a slight tug if your Sprocker Spaniel doesn't move, basically to get the pup's attention, but in most cases your pup will come right to you. Make sure you give plenty of praise. Whatever you do, do not drag your Sprocker Spaniel to you, it will immediately dig in its paws and resist and come to look upon training as a punishment.

2. **"Sit"**. An easy way to teach your Sprocker Spaniel to sit will involve the use of a treat, as well as a leash. Hold the leash close to the Sprocker Spaniel's collar and hold the treat right above its nose. Move the treat towards your Sprocker Spaniel's back. Because it cannot back up due to the control of the leash, your pup will be forced to sit. As soon as this is accomplished, say 'Sit' and treat. You can also use the command when you see your Sprocker Spaniel sitting already; give the command and treat and praise. If you use either of these methods, it will not be necessary to force your Sprocker Spaniel's hindquarters down, which will always be met with resistance.

3. **"Stay"**. This one might be a bit more difficult, due to your Sprocker Spaniel's desire to be with you, but it's not difficult if you take it slowly. Get your pup into the 'Sit' position, then take a step back, telling your Sprocker Spaniel 'Stay'. If your it remains sitting, you can treat and then take another step back, repeating "Stay' again. Don't be discouraged if this takes a bit longer for your pup to master than 'Come' or 'Sit' because of your Sprocker Spaniel's natural inclination to be with you. To begin with, you should expect your Sprocker Spaniel to break the command fairly readily. As your pup comes to understand the command, you should increase the distance between the both of you.

4. **"Down"**. 'Down' can also be somewhat difficult for your Sprocker Spaniel to master because it immediately puts your pup in a subordinate, vulnerable position. This command is useful not only for tricks, but also for keeping your Sprocker Spaniel under control in public places or around children. Shoving

your pup down or using the leash to pull your Sprocker Spaniel down is going to make it fearful, there are much better ways to accomplish this. One of the best is ways is to get your pup into a 'Sit', hold a treat in front of its nose, and gradually lower the treat to the floor. As soon as the pup is lying down, say 'Down' and reward. If you find more resistance to this command than to the others, just keep at it, with short sessions.

Some Sprocker Spaniels will be more likely to learn this if you place a pad on the floor first, it simply makes it more comfortable to lie down. You Sprocker Spaniel should learn 'Down' more quickly if you get yourself down to its level by kneeling or squatting. Keeping your face near theirs while doing this helps too.

Note: If your Sprocker Spaniel nips at your face when you bring it close, contact a dog behaviorist immediately; your pup is probably exhibiting fear aggression and this could develop into a serious problem.

5. **"Leave It" or "No"**. All of us who own Sprocker Spaniels have been faced with situations where they have picked up something awful or dangerous from the ground, and we fear that we may not be able to get to them quickly enough to remove it from their mouth. However, it's not very hard to teach your Sprocker Spaniel how to leave something alone, and learning this could prevent it from becoming ill or even dying. Sprocker Spaniels can try to eat dangerous things such as bones, dead animals, or garbage.

It's not unknown, unfortunately, for poison to be left out for dogs, or rodents that have been poisoned can kill your Sprocker Spaniel if it eats one (most rodenticides cause the mouse or rat to want to get outside which will make the corpse available to your pet).

For this lesson, you will need a leash and some treats. Leash your Sprocker Spaniel, holding the leash close to your side, then place a treat on the floor several feet from your pup. When your Sprocker Spaniel makes a move towards the treat, hold the leash firmly and say 'Leave It' or 'No'. Use a peremptory tone of voice, without shouting, to give this command. Give your pup a treat if it refrains from going towards the lure, then put another treat down on the floor. Use toys as well as treats to train your Sprocker Spaniel. Once your pup has mastered this step, you can tell it 'No' or 'Leave It' when it has something in its mouth, and by this point your Sprocker Spaniel should release whatever it is. Be sure to praise your pooch for every success and ignore any missteps. We always have used 'No' because it's short and sharp and gets your Sprocker Spaniel's attention right away; I think it rather resembles the peremptory bark that a pup might get from its mother when it was doing something unwanted.

Once you have completed your Sprocker Spaniel's basic training, you should go to the more advanced obedience command 'Heel'. While this can be somewhat difficult to teach your pooch, it will also be invaluable not only with dog tricks, but also with games and agility.

6. **"Heel"**. 'Heel' is usually considered to be the hardest basic obedience command to teach your pet. All of us have had the joy of being dragged along by an overly enthusiastic dog, and it can sometimes feel as if your arm is going to be pulled out of its socket. Not only does this take the fun out of walks for the human partner, but can also make it more likely that your Sprocker Spaniel will get in trouble with another dog or a person. Do not try to teach 'Heel' with one of those retractable dog leashes, use a leather or nylon leash that is approximately 6" long.

Do not use a choke or prong collar, a flat collar is all that is needed; you can seriously damage your Sprocker Spaniel's throat using prong or choke collars. Stand with your Sprocker Spaniel on your left side and start to walk, say 'Heel'. Keep the leash short, with your left hand exerting leash control and holding the excess length of leash in your right hand. Stop walking as soon as your Sprocker Spaniel begins to pull, even a little bit. No corrective is needed other than a cessation of motion. Don't jerk the leash or yell, just wait until your Sprocker Spaniel is motionless.

Join your pup and start walking again, repeating the procedure as needed. In most cases, you will have to repeat this many, many times. It can sometimes help to put a little piece of tape on the outside of your left leg to draw your Sprocker Spaniel's attention. Eventually your pooch will walk calmly at your side without pulling.

Now that you and your Sprocker Spaniel have gotten the framework of obedience done, you can probably begin to get going on easy-to-learn tricks for your adult or puppy Sprocker Spaniel. Dogs in general like to please their masters, so your Sprocker Spaniel will probably be more than willing to work with you to learn tricks. If you are having any problem with basic obedience training, or simply want to help your adult or puppy Sprocker Spaniel become socialized, classes are available that can help with these issues.

Always keep in mind that your Sprocker Spaniel will need 'refreshers' in all of these commands to keep them current.

Chapter Five: Easy Tricks for Your Puppy or Adult Sprocker Spaniel

Now that your Sprocker Spaniel puppy or adult has gotten all the basics down, you can start in on teaching easy tricks. Rather than jumping right to elaborate tricks, regardless of how exciting they may look, beginning with easy, simple tricks will get your Sprocker Spaniel used to learning these new maneuvers and many easy tricks will turn out to be the foundation for more difficult ones. It goes without saying, that if you are using a clicker, to click and treat after every correct response.

Easy Trick 1

Shake

This is one of the easiest tricks to teach and uses one of your Sprocker Spaniel's natural gestures.

1. The first thing to do is to get your Sprocker Spaniel into the 'Sit' position, treat, and praise. Many Sprocker Spaniels will automatically offer you their paw, and if yours does this, take advantage immediately by taking the paw and saying 'Shake'.

2. If your Sprocker Spaniel does not lift its paw automatically, squat down and hold your hand out. More than likely, at some point your pup will move its paw upwards in some way, and this is your cue to take advantage of the situation by taking the paw in your hand and saying 'Shake'.

3. Once your Sprocker Spaniel understands that you will take its paw if it raises it, you can progress to holding out your hand and giving the 'Shake' command. Most dogs will catch on quickly and be sure to treat and praise.

Easy Trick 2

Stack

Most Sprocker Spaniel puppies and adults will 'Stack' by putting both front legs onto an elevated object; perhaps your leg, or maybe the arm of the sofa. If you see your pup in this position, immediately say 'Stack' and reward and treat. If your Sprocker Spaniel doesn't stack on its own, it's easy to teach it to do so.

1. Call your Sprocker Spaniel over to you while sitting on the floor.

2. Pat your leg to encourage your Sprocker Spaniel to touch it with its paw. Treat and praise. Continue to treat and praise every time your Sprocker Spaniel puts its paw onto your leg.

3. Point to your leg now. Your Sprocker Spaniel should put both front paws onto your leg at this point. Say 'Stack' and reward your Sprocker Spaniel.

4. Practice stacking not only with your legs, but also with other objects, such as bricks or books or even an old cookie or candy tin.

5. The final step will be when you can point to an object and say 'Stack' and your Sprocker Spaniel puts both front paws up onto the object. If your Sprocker Spaniel simply seems to be unable to understand what you want, place its front legs where you want them and say 'Stack'.

Easy Trick 3

Jump

Teaching your Sprocker Spaniel to 'Jump' will lay the foundation of more difficult tricks and will also be necessary if you are interested in agility training. The length of your Sprocker Spaniel's legs will determine the maximum height it will be able to jump. Keep your Sprocker Spaniel on a short lead to begin with, although you will dispense with this later.

1. It's best to incrementalize, starting with a stick or bar either on the ground or placed only an inch or two above it. Trot with your Sprocker Spaniel to the bar and lead it over, saying 'Jump' as you do so. Don't be discouraged if your Sprocker Spaniel knocks into the bar to begin with.

2. As your Sprocker Spaniel comes to understand the lesson, you can raise the bar to make the trick more challenging. Every time your Sprocker Spaniel approaches the bar, say 'Jump'. Once your Sprocker Spaniel has learned the trick, remove the lead and let your Sprocker Spaniel jump on its own.

3. You can upgrade this trick by using a hoop: start with the hoop on the ground and gradually raise it, using the 'Jump' command every time your Sprocker Spaniel approaches the hoop. Jumping through a loop you make with your arms is another variation on this theme.

Easy Trick 4

Fetch

All dogs have prey drive, which means that they want to chase and catch what would potentially be food. 'Fetch' uses this prey drive to stimulate your Sprocker Spaniel to go after a designated object and then bring it back to you.

1. Toss one of your Sprocker Spaniel's toys, point to it, and say 'Fetch'. Most Sprocker Spaniels will be eager to go after the toy. Assuming yours does run to the toy and picks it up, praise and treat. If your Sprocker Spaniel just looks at the toy, run after it yourself, it will help to excite it and show it what is needed. Don't move on to the next step until your Sprocker Spaniel connects the word 'Fetch' with running after the toy.

2. Assuming your Sprocker Spaniel has picked up the toy, say 'Come' to bring your Sprocker Spaniel to you.

3. Once your Sprocker Spaniel is in front of you, say 'Give'. Your Sprocker Spaniel will probably not simply relinquish the toy, so have a treat ready to offer in exchange. Do not engage in a tug of war over the toy. Hand feeding of your Sprocker Spaniel, from the time it was a puppy will make it much more likely that the toy will be released without fuss, as your Sprocker Spaniel will be used to having your hands near its mouth (hand feeding greatly reduces food aggression, too).

Easy Trick 5

Give

Mentioned in the trick above, 'Give' will be much easier to teach if you have been hand feeding your puppy or adult Sprocker Spaniel. Isolating your Sprocker Spaniel with a dish when it's kibble time only fosters feelings of possessiveness in your Sprocker Spaniel and makes it less likely that it will relinquish objects from its mouth. When hand feeding your puppy or adult Sprocker Spaniel, take the food out of its mouth every so often, praising the pup for letting you do so and immediately giving the tidbit back.

We have hand fed our Sprocker Spaniels from their puppy days and have never had a problem in taking things from their mouths if necessary (even food) and have never been bitten by them either, and not a hint of a growl. If you have a Sprocker Spaniel that already suffers from food aggression or bites when you get near its food, see your veterinarian or an animal behaviorist before working on 'Give'.

1. Throw a toy and tell your Sprocker Spaniel to 'Fetch'.

2. Once your Sprocker Spaniel has the toy, say 'Come'.

3. When your Sprocker Spaniel has come to you, take the toy while saying 'Give'. Holding a treat up to your Sprocker Spaniel's nose will prompt it to open its mouth to get the treat, thereby releasing the toy. Give your Sprocker Spaniel the treat and praise it.

4. Repeat these steps several times until your Sprocker Spaniel allows you to take the object out of its mouth without problem; keep the treat in sight, and smell, and your Sprocker Spaniel will be happy for you to remove the object.

Easy Trick 6

Drop

This is built on the above 'Give' trick. As soon as your Sprocker Spaniel gives you whatever it has fetched reliably, you can move on to 'Drop'.

1. Follow the 'Fetch' sequence.

2. When your Sprocker Spaniel brings the object to you, don't take it out of its mouth.

3. Hold a treat to your Sprocker Spaniel's nose; sooner or later, your Sprocker Spaniel will let go of the object to get the treat.

4. As soon as the object is released, say 'Drop'. Give your Sprocker Spaniel the treat.

Easy Trick 7

Pull

This should be very easy to teach, as nearly every dog alive loves a tug-of-war.

1. Using a rope toy or just a piece of rag with a knot in it, let your Sprocker Spaniel take one end in its mouth. Tug on your end and it's almost a 100% chance that your Sprocker Spaniel will begin tugging on the other. Whenever your Sprocker Spaniel gives a

tug, say 'Pull' and praise. This trick will come in useful for more involved tricks.

2. Tie the rag or rope onto a door handle and show it to your Sprocker Spaniel. If you've been playing tug-of-war with your Sprocker Spaniel it will probably take the rag into its mouth, if not, hold the rag out to it.

3. As soon as your Sprocker Spaniel has the cloth in its mouth, say 'Pull'. Treat your Sprocker Spaniel as soon as it pulls even a little bit. This trick is useful not only for opening doors, but can also be used for fetching cans from the fridge.

Easy Trick 8

Sit Pretty (Beg)

Certainly one of the old favorites, you'll find it isn't very difficult to teach your Sprocker Spaniel to 'Sit Pretty'. If you haven't taught your Sprocker Spaniel to 'Sit', you will have to go back and teach that before starting this trick.

1. Tell your Sprocker Spaniel to 'Sit'.

2. Hold a treat in front of your Sprocker Spaniel's nose and slowly raise it up higher. If your Sprocker Spaniel breaks the 'Sit', start over again.

3. As your Sprocker Spaniel tries to get the treat, it will position itself in an upright sitting position, with its front legs off the ground. Give your Sprocker Spaniel the treat now. Repeat this until your Sprocker Spaniel does it reliably.

4. Now it's time to add the command. You may want to use either 'Beg' or 'Pretty' so as to avoid confusion with the 'Sit' command. Chose one command and use it consistently. Make certain to treat your Sprocker Spaniel as soon as it performs the trick reliably as well as praising your Sprocker Spaniel verbally. You can dispense

with the treat once your Sprocker Spaniel responds correctly, but continue with verbal praise.

Easy Trick 9

Crawl

This trick will actually come in handy later on if you want to participate in agility with your Sprocker Spaniel, and could help your Sprocker Spaniel master the both the open and collapsed tunnel.

1. Tell your Sprocker Spaniel 'Down'.

2. Put a treat on the floor in front of your Sprocker Spaniel, about 1 foot away, but cover it with your hand.

3. Lift up your hand a bit to show your Sprocker Spaniel the treat and say 'Crawl'. To begin with, your Sprocker Spaniel will undoubtedly jump up to get the treat. Return it to the 'Down' position and hide a treat beneath your hand again.

4. Keeping your hand hovering over the treat will help keep your Sprocker Spaniel's interest close to the ground and more likely to scoot along in a crawl rather than get up.

5. As soon as your Sprocker Spaniel is actually crawling towards the treat, pull it back further to keep it crawling. If your Sprocker Spaniel gets back onto its feet at this stage, it could be because you are pulling the treat back too quickly. Slow down until your Sprocker Spaniel really gets the hang of the trick.

Easy Trick 10

Nose Balance

This is a fairly easy trick to teach most Sprocker Spaniels. However, you may be presented with some challenges at times but remember that the secret to success is patience and perseverance. Before starting actual training, make sure that your Sprocker Spaniel is comfortable with you putting your hands on its muzzle. If this is fairly new to your puppy or adult Sprocker Spaniel, take a bit of time to make sure your pup isn't skittish when something comes near its face; instinct tells your Sprocker Spaniel that that is where the teeth are. Once that has been accomplished, you can begin to teach the trick. You can use treats or objects as the balancing item, although your Sprocker Spaniel would probably prefer the treat.

1. 'Sit' followed by 'Stay' is a good way to begin. Praise your Sprocker Spaniel.

2. If you are using an object, make sure that it's lightweight. Place the treat or object close to your Sprocker Spaniel's stop, which will help to hold it in place; it's probably better not to start with a ball which might just roll off your Sprocker Spaniel's nose. Treat and praise. Use the cue 'Balance'.

3. Leave the object on your Sprocker Spaniel's nose for only a few seconds and remove it before your Sprocker Spaniel starts to act uncomfortable.

4. You can leave the object on for longer and longer periods as your Sprocker Spaniel becomes used to it. Always remember to give a treat and praise your Sprocker Spaniel, and never leave the object on for an extended period of time.

Easy Trick 11

Speak

This trick is not only easy to teach your Sprocker Spaniel, but can also help to prevent nuisance barking as your pup will learn only to bark when told to do so.

1. As soon as your puppy or adult Sprocker Spaniel barks, say 'Speak' and praise and treat.

2. Repeat this step and then try giving the command while your pup is quiet.

3. If you are lucky enough to have a very quiet Sprocker Spaniel, you can often get it to bark by introducing a strange noise, such as someone pounding on the front door or shouting outside. This will often stimulate your Sprocker Spaniel's protective instincts enough to cause it to bark.

4. As your Sprocker Spaniel comes to understand the 'Speak' command, put your Sprocker Spaniel into 'Sit' before giving it. This will make it easier to teach more difficult tricks later on.

Easy Trick 12

Bow

This trick takes advantage of your Sprocker Spaniel's natural invitation to play. When dogs want to play with you or just another dog, they lower their front quarters while leaving their rear up in the air. Just build on this inclination to have your Sprocker Spaniel 'Bowing' on cue.

1. Wait until you see your Sprocker Spaniel in the play position and say 'Bow' and treat.

2. Every time your Sprocker Spaniel indicates it wants to play, say 'Bow' and give your Sprocker Spaniel a treat.

3. After several repetitions, try saying 'Bow' while your Sprocker Spaniel is simply standing in front of you. Don't expect a correct response immediately, although some Sprocker Spaniels might surprise you.

4. If your Sprocker Spaniel simply doesn't seem to get the message, try leading its front quarters down to the ground by holding a treat in front of its nose and lowering it to the floor.

5. In case your Sprocker Spaniel goes into the 'Down' position with its entire body on the floor, have a helper hold its hindquarters

up while the front are lowering. Remember to say 'Bow' as you work on this and don't stint on treats and praise.

Easy Trick 13

Salute

This is another easy trick that is based on your Sprocker Spaniel's natural actions. Keep in mind that this 'Salute' will be performed with one of the hind legs. This is an amusing trick that I taught to our male Sprocker Spaniel, and he developed real pride in kicking out his right hind leg and holding it there in a very nice salute. As you know, most Sprocker Spaniels will kick at the ground with their hind legs after going to the bathroom, and it is just this action that you will be using to teach your Sprocker Spaniel to salute.

Both male and female Sprocker Spaniels can learn this without much trouble, and from my experience, they seem to enjoy doing it, too. This might be a good trick if you have a family member returning from military service; he or she will probably be delighted to be greeted with a salute.

1. After your Sprocker Spaniel has finished its business and has started to kick out, say 'Salute'. Treat your Sprocker Spaniel.

2. Repeat this command every time your Sprocker Spaniel does it, and it won't be very long before your Sprocker Spaniel comes to associate the word with the action.

3. Once your Sprocker Spaniel seems to connect the word with kicking out its hind leg, give the 'Salute' command. Undoubtedly your Sprocker Spaniel will not understand what you want, but repeat the command several times. Don't overdo this, if there isn't success after 2 or 3 tries, leave off for the time being, and wait for the next trip outside.

4. Any slight quiver of the hind leg should be looked upon as a victory and rewarded. It should not be too long before your Sprocker Spaniel will give you a salute upon command.

Easy Trick 14

Spin

Spinning is something like a dog chasing its tail, but instead of it being a spontaneous action, it is now a trick to be done upon cue. Some dogs actually spin naturally, we had a dog quite some time ago who would spin around in circles when she got excited.

1. Hold a treat right in front of your Sprocker Spaniel's nose.

2. Move the treat towards your Sprocker Spaniel's right shoulder, keeping it as close as possible to its body. Your Sprocker Spaniel should turn in a tight circling motion to try to get the treat.

3. Keep moving the treat around until you have completed a complete rotation, then say 'Spin' and give your Sprocker Spaniel the treat.

4. Use this same procedure to have your Sprocker Spaniel go around several times, slowly at first, then upping the speed. Remember to tell your Sprocker Spaniel to 'Spin' as you move the treat.

5. Try causing your Sprocker Spaniel to move simply by moving your hand the same way you moved the treat, your Sprocker Spaniel will probably just follow your hand.

6. This is a good treat to teach using both verbal and hand signals. In addition to saying 'Spin', you can also make a circular motion with your hand. Before long your Sprocker Spaniel will probably be spinning away just on command. Always remember to treat and praise.

Easy Trick 15

High Five

This might be looked upon as the modern world's 'Shake' and is just as easy to teach as shake is. It utilizes your Sprocker Spaniel's natural inclination to paw at things, and might be very amusing if you have two dogs and they are taught to 'High Five' one another. This trick depends on utilizing your Sprocker Spaniel's sense of smell to get results, so be sure to have some highly odorous treats that your Sprocker Spaniel really likes, such as a piece of meat or cheese ready.

1. Put your Sprocker Spaniel into the 'Sit' position and give a treat.

2. Place one of the treats into your hand and make a fist. Even though your Sprocker Spaniel will not be able to see the treat, it will certainly be able to smell it.

3. Put your hand in front of your Sprocker Spaniel, slightly below its nose. Your hand should be only a few inches from your Sprocker Spaniel at this point.

4. Inevitably, your Sprocker Spaniel will try to sniff at your hand to get the treat, but you should totally ignore this. Don't even say 'No'.

5. When attempting to sniff gets no results, most Sprocker Spaniels will paw at your hand. Give your Sprocker Spaniel the treat and praise it.

6. Repeat the above step until your Sprocker Spaniel consistently paws at your fist, rather than sniffing at it.

7. Now, open your hand, keeping the palm up and hold it just where you were holding your fist. Most Sprocker Spaniels will paw at your open hand. If your Sprocker Spaniel doesn't, then just go back to the fist, but with nothing in it, until your Sprocker

Spaniel paws at your open hand. You may well have to go back and forth several times.

8. Once your Sprocker Spaniel is pawing reliably at your open palm, put it into the correct position for a high five. As soon as your Sprocker Spaniel taps your palm, say 'High Five' and treat. It shouldn't be long before all your Sprocker Spaniel has to do to give you a 'High Five' is to see your palm presented.

Easy Trick 16

Kiss

As long as you don't mind getting licked on your face, this is a rather endearing and easy trick to teach to your Sprocker Spaniel. Make sure that your Sprocker Spaniel is comfortable having your face close to its face, some Sprocker Spaniels are skittish about this, especially if you have a Sprocker Spaniel that you adopted as an adult. However, as long as you don't mind your Sprocker Spaniel's tongue and breath, and both of you are calm when in close proximity, you may enjoy learning this trick.

Keep in mind that even if you enjoy getting a big, juicy kiss from your Sprocker Spaniel, visitors or other family members may not find the trick to be very amusing, so ask the other person whether or not they do want a kiss from your Sprocker Spaniel before directing your Sprocker Spaniel to do so.

1. Put a small smear of something like strawberry jam, peanut butter, or gravy on your cheek or even the end of your nose.

2. Put your face at the level of your Sprocker Spaniel's face. Your Sprocker Spaniel will, of course, be attracted to the lure and lick.

3. When your Sprocker Spaniel does lick your face, say 'Kiss'. This will probably be one of the easiest tricks to teach your Sprocker Spaniel, and you will soon be able to dispense with the lure and just rely on the cue to get results.

4. Depending on how liquid your Sprocker Spaniel's mouth is, you may want to have a tissue ready to mop up after the kiss.

These basic, easy-to-learn and easy-to-teach tricks can now form the foundation of more difficult tricks to teach your Sprocker Spaniel. You and your Sprocker Spaniel are now very comfortable working with one another and are really functioning as a team. Of course, if you are satisfied with this level, it's perfectly acceptable to remain here, there is nothing to demand that you go on to tricks of an intermediate difficulty, the whole point is to have fun with your Sprocker Spaniel, not to be in any kind of competition.

Chapter Six: Progressing to Intermediate Level Tricks

Hopefully you and your puppy or adult Sprocker Spaniel have had a lot of fun learning the easy tricks, and both of you might well be eager to get started on intermediate tricks. These will add a bit of complexity and interest, but are not beyond the ability of most Sprocker Spaniels to learn.

Teaching your Sprocker Spaniel obedience and then easy tricks will not only have strengthened the bond between you, but both of you will be able to work more effectively as a team – you have both learned to respond to one another more effectively, picking up even subtle cues of facial expression or body language. Intermediate tricks will add another dimension to your Sprocker Spaniel's activities, and the challenge they pose will help to keep your Sprocker Spaniel stimulated and engaged.

Intermediate Trick 1

Push

'Push' is the mirror image of 'Pull' and your Sprocker Spaniel can be taught to do this using its nose or its paws. Adult Sprocker Spaniels may prefer to use their paws, while the smaller puppy Sprocker Spaniels will probably prefer to use their nose (or head). There's no set rule for this so you are free to experiment. Our Sprocker Spaniels always used their heads to butt the door either open or closed. Using this trick, you can train your Sprocker Spaniel to close the door after it comes inside, which is handy at all seasons.

1. You will need to establish a target, such as a small toy or a piece of cloth or paper.

2. Offer the target to your Sprocker Spaniel, allowing your Sprocker Spaniel to sniff it. Tap your finger on the target so that your Sprocker Spaniel will come to associate the sound with the target. Some dogs may paw at it, which is perfectly fine, too. Treat your Sprocker Spaniel. Repeat this until your Sprocker Spaniel will come to the target and touch it reliably.

3. The next step will be to attach the target to a door. Tape the toy, cloth, or paper onto the door at the appropriate level. Tap the target. The door should be just slightly open.

4. Show your Sprocker Spaniel the target, tap the target, and motion your Sprocker Spaniel to go to the door. As soon as your Sprocker Spaniel's nose or paw touches the target, say 'Push'. At this point, it doesn't matter if the door moves or not. Praise your Sprocker Spaniel and treat.

5. You will have to repeat this several times, opening the door a bit wider every time you work at this trick.

6. As your Sprocker Spaniel becomes more adept at this, remove the target and simply tap the door, saying 'Push' as you do so. Treat and praise as soon as your Sprocker Spaniel touches the door.

7. The next step is to tell your Sprocker Spaniel to 'Push' without any other cues than your voice. Stand near the door to get your Sprocker Spaniel to come. By this time, your Sprocker Spaniel will probably understand enough to go to the door and push it closed.

8. Finally, you should be able to give your Sprocker Spaniel the command wherever you are in the room and it will go to the door and close it.

Intermediate Trick 2

Play Dead

This is one of the favorite tricks to teach your Sprocker Spaniel, but is also one where you might encounter some resistance because your Sprocker Spaniel will feel vulnerable. Trust in you has nothing to do with this, it is purely an instinctive reaction, honed by eons of living in the wild. Be patient and calm to help build your Sprocker Spaniel's confidence and trust. You can use both verbal and visual cues for this trick.

1. Give the 'Down' command, either while your Sprocker Spaniel is standing or sitting. Most Sprocker Spaniels will tend to lean one way or another while lying down, so take advantage of this if your Sprocker Spaniel is leaning to the left or right. Praise and treat. Pet your Sprocker Spaniel to help it relax.

2. Once your Sprocker Spaniel seems relaxed, gently push it over onto its side. If your Sprocker Spaniel seems to be panicking, stop immediately and try again after a break. Lying down next to your Sprocker Spaniel can sometimes help it to comply.

3. After a number of repetitions, your Sprocker Spaniel will be able to go from a 'Down' into lying on its side with no problem.

4. Choose the verbal cue for your Sprocker Spaniel, it can be 'You're dead' or 'Play dead'. You can even add a physical cue such as making a chopping motion or holding your hand like a gun.

Intermediate Trick 3

Roll Over

Like 'Play Dead', 'Roll Over' involves using the 'Down' command to begin the trick. You can teach a hand signal while teaching the verbal one, simply make a rolling motion with your hand while cuing your Sprocker Spaniel.

1. Tell your Sprocker Spaniel 'Down'. Praise and treat.

2. Use a treat to draw your Sprocker Spaniel's attention over one of its shoulders – your Sprocker Spaniel's nose will follow the smell.

3. Keep moving the treat farther and farther over, towards your Sprocker Spaniel's back until your Sprocker Spaniel is on its side. Praise and treat.

4. Follow through with the momentum of the treat to encourage your Sprocker Spaniel to roll over onto its back and then onto its other side. At this point say 'Roll Over' and give your Sprocker Spaniel the treat.

5. Several repetitions will teach your Sprocker Spaniel this trick and you can soon dispense with the treat and rely on your verbal command.

Intermediate Trick 4

Get Your Leash

This intermediate trick uses 'Fetch' as its foundation. Don't be surprised, once your Sprocker Spaniel has learned this trick, if it doesn't bring the leash to you unbidden to ask for a walk, however.

1. Place the leash on the floor, step back, and wait for your Sprocker Spaniel to investigate. Praise your Sprocker Spaniel as soon as it noses the leash.

2. Tell your Sprocker Spaniel 'Fetch' and praise and treat when the leash is taken into the mouth.

3. Encourage your Sprocker Spaniel to come to you by slapping your legs or making 'chucking' sounds.

4. When your Sprocker Spaniel brings the leash over to you, praise it, say 'Leash' and treat as soon as your Sprocker Spaniel releases the leash into your hands.

5. You can eliminate the 'Fetch' command and the encouragement for your Sprocker Spaniel to come as soon as your Sprocker Spaniel brings the leash to you reliably, and simply rely on telling your Sprocker Spaniel 'Leash' when it's time for a walk.

Intermediate Trick 5

Play the Piano

No, you won't get any virtuoso performances out of your pup, but you can teach it to plunk away on the piano. Use a bench for your Sprocker Spaniel to sit on, rather than trying to balance on a piano stool, and a padded bench will help with stability.

1. The first step is to teach your Sprocker Spaniel to tap on something with its paws. You can use a disc toy or even a folded up towel. Tell your Sprocker Spaniel 'Sit' and place the target on the floor in front of your Sprocker Spaniel and touch it with your hand.

2. If your Sprocker Spaniel tries to sniff at where you are touching, ignore this and pull your hand away. Try tapping the target until your Sprocker Spaniel places its paw on it. At this point, be sure to treat and praise.

3. Use the phrase 'Play the Piano' whenever your Sprocker Spaniel taps on the target.

4. Gradually make the target smaller (it will have to be small enough to be placed on the keys of the piano). Use the lid from a small food container or fold up a washcloth.

5. Once your Sprocker Spaniel taps on the smaller target reliably every time you use the cue phrase, it's time to get your pianist to the keyboard.

6. Sit next to your Sprocker Spaniel on the bench to help it feel relaxed and place the target on the keys.

7. Say 'Play the Piano' to get your Sprocker Spaniel to strike on the target. Your Sprocker Spaniel might be a bit startled at the sound to begin with, but most Sprocker Spaniels will accommodate themselves quickly.

8. As soon as your Sprocker Spaniel is striking the target upon command, remove the target and just let your Sprocker Spaniel hit the keys with its paws.

9. One-pawed playing can be expanded to two-pawed playing by putting the target on the keyboard while the first paw is already engaged. Your Sprocker Spaniel will probably catch on quickly to this addition.

Intermediate Trick 6

Leg Weaving

This is fun to do on its own, but will also come in handy if you are interested in agility training. The first thing to do is to train yourself to take long strides – your Sprocker Spaniel will have to move through your legs.

If your Sprocker Spaniel is on the larger side, you can still do this trick by holding one leg out in front of you, bent at the knee, with the foot above the ground. If using this latter technique, you will step down with the foot you had raised, then raise the other one instead and take a long step with that one, too. Once you have gotten your stride down, it's time to start working with your Sprocker Spaniel.

1. Position your Sprocker Spaniel on your left, then take a step forward on your right foot to form a tunnel or arch for your Sprocker Spaniel with your right leg.

2. Hold a treat on the other side of your right leg to get your Sprocker Spaniel to travel through. Say 'Weave' as your Sprocker Spaniel does so. Praise your pup now.

3. Give your Sprocker Spaniel the treat and repeat the instruction using the left leg as the tunnel.

4. Go slowly at first, then gradually increase your striding as your Sprocker Spaniel progresses.

5. With patience, your Sprocker Spaniel will soon be able to weave through your legs as you walk along at a normal pace.

Intermediate Trick 7

Hind Legs Stand

One of our Sprocker Spaniels, and his son, had a natural talent for standing on their hind legs and walking backwards. Both Sprocker Spaniels could navigate a room in reverse with no problem. This was evidently a genetic trait since neither of them had to be taught how to do this, but would do it spontaneously. However, even if your Sprocker Spaniel doesn't have this particular gene, you can teach it to get up onto its hind legs and even walk, either forwards or backwards.

An important thing to keep in mind here is to make sure your Sprocker Spaniel's hips are healthy. Sprocker Spaniels with arthritis or dysplasia should not be taught this trick, it will simply be painful and could make the condition worse. It's probably a good idea to have your veterinarian check your Sprocker Spaniel over, especially its hips and back before starting to teach this trick. Generally, the smaller Sprocker Spaniels have an easier time learning this, but literally any hip healthy Sprocker Spaniel can learn to stand on its hind legs.

1. Tell your Sprocker Spaniel to 'Sit'.

2. Hold a treat above your Sprocker Spaniel's nose and raise it up directly above your Sprocker Spaniel's head. Raising the treat straight up will prevent your Sprocker Spaniel from backing up to try to get the treat.

3. Your Sprocker Spaniel will first sit up on its hind legs, then will raise itself onto its hind feet to reach the treat. Say 'Stand Up' and give your Sprocker Spaniel a treat. You can add a hand signal, gesturing upwards when you give the verbal command.

4. As your Sprocker Spaniel responds to this trick, you can start teaching it to walk towards you while on its hind legs. Holding a treat just above your Sprocker Spaniel's nose and walking slowly backwards will get your Sprocker Spaniel walking upright.

5. Don't overdo this; the muscles in your Sprocker Spaniel's legs and back that keep it upright have to strengthen, and your Sprocker Spaniel's sense of balance must adjust to this new trick.

6. Some Sprocker Spaniels can eventually learn to walk on their back legs for long periods of time and can even learn to dance. It is not unusual to see a Sprocker Spaniel that can dance on its hind legs for several minutes without problem.

Intermediate Trick 8

Find

This trick actually involves 3 steps – 'Sniff', 'Find', and 'Fetch'. 'Sniff', of course, is the easier to teach, but is necessary to proceed on to 'Find'. You will need some treats and whatever object you want your Sprocker Spaniel to find.

As you can see, the tricks are now becoming more complex and challenging, but learning this trick is necessary if you wish to train your Sprocker Spaniel for complicated tricks and tasks in the home.

1. Tell your Sprocker Spaniel to 'Sit'. Hold onto its collar or keep it on leash.

2. Present a treat in front of your Sprocker Spaniel's nose and say 'Sniff'. Don't let your Sprocker Spaniel take the treat.

3. Throw the treat several feet away on the floor, telling your Sprocker Spaniel to 'Stay' to prevent its going right for the treat.

4. Undoubtedly, your Sprocker Spaniel's eyes are riveted on the treat, so release your Sprocker Spaniel and say 'Find'. At this point, your Sprocker Spaniel will not yet associate the command with the action, but several repetitions will serve to teach this trick.

5. Once your Sprocker Spaniel has made the connection between the 'Find' command and going to the treat you can lengthen the distance.

6. Substitute an object for the treat now. Show the object to your Sprocker Spaniel and toss it 4 or 5 feet away. Say 'Find' and release your Sprocker Spaniel. As soon as your Sprocker Spaniel has found the object, say 'Fetch' so that your Sprocker Spaniel will bring it to you.

7. Gradually increase the distance until it has reached a point where your Sprocker Spaniel will not be able to visually find the object.

8. Now it's time to place the object where your Sprocker Spaniel cannot see it. You should begin this by leaving the object on the floor, where your Sprocker Spaniel will come upon it just by walking towards it. The next step will be to conceal the object behind furniture, and then proceed to placing the object in another room.

9. Once the object is out of sight, tell your Sprocker Spaniel to 'Find' and then give the command to 'Fetch'. As long as your Sprocker Spaniel is enjoying itself, this will not be an overly difficult trick for your Sprocker Spaniel to learn.

Intermediate Trick 9

Quiet

Nuisance barking is just that – a nuisance. While barking in your home can be irritating enough, if you live in an apartment house, it could get you evicted if the other tenants are annoyed sufficiently. Even if you live in a detached home, neighbors who live close to you can still be irritated by your barking Sprocker Spaniel, especially if you leave your pooch outside for long periods of time. Your home will be a lot quieter and more peaceful if you teach your Sprocker Spaniel the 'Quiet' command.

If you are interested in teaching your Sprocker Spaniel to be 'Quiet', you are probably getting tired of listening to nonstop barking that can go on almost interminably. Screaming at your Sprocker Spaniel won't help - your Sprocker Spaniel may well think you're just joining in the fun. Once again, like many undesirable behaviors, barking often arises when your Sprocker Spaniel is bored, so working with your Sprocker Spaniel on this in a positive way will ultimately make both of you happier.

1. If you have a problem barker, you probably won't have any difficulty in catching your Sprocker Spaniel in the act. Make sure you have plenty of treats on hand and if you are using a clicker, get ready to click.

2. As soon as there is a break in the barking, praise your Sprocker Spaniel and give it a treat. Do not say anything to your Sprocker Spaniel while it's barking.

3. Your Sprocker Spaniel will soon come to associate a treat with a cessation of barking.

4. Now is the time to introduce the 'Quiet' command, when your Sprocker Spaniel has stopped barking and has gotten a treat.

5. After several repetitions of the above, tell your Sprocker Spaniel 'Quiet' when it's barking. Don't expect miracles the first couple of times, and continue with the rewards during times when your Sprocker Spaniel is not barking. When your Sprocker

Spaniel does stop barking when you command it to, be sure to give plenty of treats and praise.

6. The barking habit should eventually fade away as your Sprocker Spaniel gets used to not barking at all.

By now you and your Sprocker Spaniel are on the way to becoming experts and are ready to take on the more difficult tricks. Always remember that you can stop teaching tricks at any level; there is nothing that dictates that you have to continue, the point is to have fun together.

Chapter Seven: Mastering the Hard Ones

The easy and intermediate Sprocker Spaniel tricks have by now laid a solid foundation on which to advance to more difficult and complicated tricks. Both you and your Sprocker Spaniel will now be very well attuned to one another and will be working more as a partnership, rather than just master and dog.

Many of the hard tricks will encompass several stages and will involve tricks that your Sprocker Spaniel has learned already. If you and your Sprocker Spaniel have been proceeding in a positive, upbeat way, your Sprocker Spaniel will probably be eager to start working on more challenging projects.

Advanced Trick 1

Find

Now it's time to take 'Find' to the next phase where you will be teaching your Sprocker Spaniel to find specific objects. Start with one thing you want to find and then add others once your Sprocker Spaniel can reliably find the first.

1. Show your Sprocker Spaniel the object, for instance your slippers (since this seems to be a favorite), and say 'Sniff'. Repeat this several times, giving your Sprocker Spaniel a treat and some praise every time you do so.

2. Once your Sprocker Spaniel has sniffed the slippers adequately, say 'Slippers'. Help your Sprocker Spaniel associate the object with the name by treating and praising.

3. Place the slippers on the floor and say 'Find Slippers'. Hopefully your Sprocker Spaniel will go to the slippers without problem.

4. As soon as your Sprocker Spaniel has picked up one of the slippers, say 'Fetch' to have your Sprocker Spaniel bring the slipper to you. Repeat for the other slipper.

5. Follow the same procedure for any object you want your Sprocker Spaniel to bring to you. Don't overload your Sprocker Spaniel with a laundry list of items to start with, concentrate on a few until your Sprocker Spaniel performs reliably and never forget to praise your Sprocker Spaniel and give it a treat. You can teach your Sprocker Spaniel to identify and find its toys, among other things.

6. Always remember to start teaching your Sprocker Spaniel to 'Find' whatever object by placing it first in full view and gradually lengthening the distance until the object is out of sight completely and your Sprocker Spaniel has to search for it.

Advanced Trick 2

Find Can

If, after a long day at work you just want to relax in front of the television, but realize after sitting down that you don't have anything to drink, you can train your Sprocker Spaniel to bring you a can of your favorite beverage from the refrigerator. You will definitely need hands on work with your Sprocker Spaniel to get this trick down pat, but it is not impossible for a smart Sprocker Spaniel to learn, and will save your weary feet once your Sprocker Spaniel understands what is required of it.

This trick will require the use of several previous tricks including 'Find', 'Pull', 'Come', 'Push' and will require patience on your part. Because of the complexity of this trick, your Sprocker Spaniel will have to learn the proper sequence for it to be successful, so be patient and have plenty of treats on hand.

1. Tie a piece of cloth or a rag to the refrigerator handle

2. Take your Sprocker Spaniel to the refrigerator and point out the rag. Tell your Sprocker Spaniel 'Pull'. If your Sprocker Spaniel has mastered this trick, it will take the rag and pull to open

the door. As soon as the refrigerator door is open, praise your Sprocker Spaniel and treat.

3. Now, you have to familiarize your Sprocker Spaniel with the can. Take a can of beverage out of the refrigerator and put it on the floor in front of your Sprocker Spaniel. Say 'Can'. Use a cold can to get your Sprocker Spaniel used to the feel of the cold can in its mouth. Your Sprocker Spaniel may lick the can, which is perfectly all right.

4. Touch the can and say 'Find Can'. If your Sprocker Spaniel doesn't pick the can up in its mouth, put the can into your Sprocker Spaniel's mouth yourself. Do not pry open your Sprocker Spaniel's jaws to do this, chances are that your Sprocker Spaniel will just take the can when you offer it. Make sure you praise your Sprocker Spaniel as soon as the can is in its mouth.

5. Place the can in the fridge on the lowest shelf (if you use the door for cans, likewise place it on the lowest slot). Point to the can or tap it with your finger and say 'Find Can'. Once your Sprocker Spaniel will reliably take the can off the shelf, it's time for the next step.

6. Now your lessons teaching your Sprocker Spaniel to close door will come in handy as you tell your Sprocker Spaniel to 'Push' while tapping on the refrigerator door. Praise your Sprocker Spaniel.

7. Go to wherever you enjoy sitting, while your Sprocker Spaniel still has the can in its mouth and say 'Come'. Your Sprocker Spaniel should come to where you are and you can take the can out of its mouth. Be lavish with the praise.

8. This is a very difficult and involved trick to teach your Sprocker Spaniel, but it can be done as long as you are willing to put in the time and have the patience to teach it. You will need to go through the steps quite a few times with most Sprocker Spaniels.

9. Remember that your Sprocker Spaniel will have to learn that the 'Find Can' command actually is only the trigger for a number of other actions that will have to be followed.

10. Once you feel confident that your Sprocker Spaniel has mastered all the steps, sit down and tell your Sprocker Spaniel 'Find Can', then sit back and relax with a nice, cool drink.

Advanced Trick 3

Jump Rope

You can teach this in collaboration with another person to hold one end of the rope, or you can do it by yourself by tying one end of the rope to a stationary object. This is one of the hardest tricks to learn, but one that will be rewarding for both you and your Sprocker Spaniel. Don't start teaching this until your puppy has basically stopped growing as beginning too early could cause damage to the pup's hips. In order to do this trick, your Sprocker Spaniel should already know 'Jump' and 'Stand Up'. If your Sprocker Spaniel is unfamiliar with these, go back and teach these first.

Where you conduct your lessons will depend upon the size/age of your Sprocker Spaniel. For your smaller pooch, you could place it on a table to make it easier for both of you, and for a larger one, you could teach your lesson on the floor.

Place a small rug with low pile and rubber backing (a bathmat works very well) on the table or a bare floor to provide good traction for your Sprocker Spaniel's feet. It might also be a good idea to make sure that your Sprocker Spaniel's claws are adequately trimmed as long nails can get caught in rug pile and can make it hard for your Sprocker Spaniel to stand up or jump.

The only equipment you will need for this trick is a jump rope. Because of the complexity of this trick, you should have a plentiful supply of treats on hand.

1. Your Sprocker Spaniel should be introduced to the rope by swinging it back and forth in front of it. Let your Sprocker Spaniel sniff the rope, but don't let it bite it. Treat and praise.

2. Once your Sprocker Spaniel is comfortable with the moving rope, position the rope on the floor behind your Sprocker Spaniel, give it a nearly full rotation to end up stationary at your Sprocker Spaniel's front feet. At this point, say 'Jump' and as your Sprocker Spaniel jumps, move the rope beneath its feet. Praise and treat.

3. Flip the rope like this over and over, saying 'Jump' each time the rope appears in front of your Sprocker Spaniel's front feet. In time your Sprocker Spaniel will begin to jump as soon as it sees the rope approaching its feet. Once your Sprocker Spaniel has mastered this part of the instructions, it's time to move onto the next.

4. Now it's time to get your Sprocker Spaniel to stand up and jump when the rope comes around. The first thing to do is give the 'Stand Up' command. Praise and treat.

5. As you did when your Sprocker Spaniel was in a normal position, flip the rope from in back of your Sprocker Spaniel to just before its hind feet and say 'Jump'. Quickly move the rope to the back of your Sprocker Spaniel's feet (your Sprocker Spaniel is on its hind legs now, so don't linger).

6. Repeat flipping the rope and saying 'Jump' until your Sprocker Spaniel is able to do this reliably. Keep the rope jumping slow at first, and gradually speed it up as your Sprocker Spaniel gains skill and its balance improves.

Advanced Trick 4

Count

When your Sprocker Spaniel learns this trick, it will definitely look like a canine genius! This trick will combine the 'Speak' trick with eye and hand signals from you. The complicated nature of this trick means that you will probably have to spend considerable time working on it, but it will definitely amaze your friends when your Sprocker Spaniel does arithmetic for them. Remember to remain patient and stick with it.

1. Tell your Sprocker Spaniel to 'Sit' and position yourself so that your face is directly in front of your Sprocker Spaniel's face. You won't have to be this close after your Sprocker Spaniel has learned the trick.

2. Hold up your right hand while holding a treat in your left.

3. Look into your Sprocker Spaniel's right eye, making sure that you are both making eye contact with each other.

4. Tell your Sprocker Spaniel to 'Speak' and give it the treat as soon as your Sprocker Spaniel does so. Make certain that your Sprocker Spaniel is still looking you in the eye. Repeat this several times so that your Sprocker Spaniel comes to associate barking with your eye contact.

5. The next step will have you telling your Sprocker Spaniel to 'Speak', but now you will avert your eyes. Let your right hand drop down a bit, too. The point here is to let your Sprocker Spaniel know that when you let your hand fall and avert your eyes, that there is to be no more barking. Treat when your Sprocker Spaniel cooperates. Repeat this and treat whenever your Sprocker Spaniel stops barking when you avert your eyes and drop your hand.

6. Once your Sprocker Spaniel understands that one bark is sufficient when you look away, it's time to train your Sprocker Spaniel to bark twice. Position yourself as above and tell your Sprocker Spaniel to 'Speak'. Repeat the command if your Sprocker Spaniel stops after one bark. Keep eye contact until 2 barks have been given. Some Sprocker Spaniels will bark too much and some will bark too little, but by persevering, you will eventually teach your Sprocker Spaniel to cease barking as soon as you avert your eyes and drop your hand.

7. Build on the number of barks required using both eye and hand signals, always remembering to treat and praise after a success.

8. When your Sprocker Spaniel is reliably barking to your cues, stop using the hand signal and rely on your eyes only.

9. Now it's time to add the math: ask your Sprocker Spaniel how much is 1 + 1? Then tell your Sprocker Spaniel 'Speak'.

10. As soon as your Sprocker Spaniel barks twice, avert your eyes. You can use addition, subtraction, multiplication, and division to show off your Sprocker Spaniel's education, but try to keep the numbers on the low side to make it easier for your Sprocker Spaniel and make it more likely that the trick will be a success.

Advanced Trick 5

Grip Object

While you will be training your Sprocker Spaniel with a lightweight object that it can grasp easily, once your Sprocker Spaniel has learned how to grip an object, you can use any number of things, including dolls or toys. A plastic, personal-size water bottle is a good choice, but because it's slippery, you might find it easier for your Sprocker Spaniel to grip this if you tape a lightweight piece of cloth around it. You will use the word 'Grip' for this trick.

1. Show the bottle to your Sprocker Spaniel and praise as soon as your Sprocker Spaniel touches its nose to the bottle. This will familiarize your Sprocker Spaniel with the object.

2. Repeat this until your Sprocker Spaniel lifts its paw to touch the bottle. Holding the bottle just slightly out and down a bit will encourage your Sprocker Spaniel to use its paw. Treat your Sprocker Spaniel when it touches the bottle with its paw.

3. Tap the bottle on the inside of your Sprocker Spaniel's leg when it raises its paw, then press the bottle against your Sprocker

Spaniel's chest. Say 'Grip'. You should still keep your hand on the bottle at this point to prevent your Sprocker Spaniel simply dropping it. You will undoubtedly have to repeat this step several times until your Sprocker Spaniel understands to hold the bottle against its chest.

4. The next step will involve removing your hand from the bottle once your Sprocker Spaniel has taken it. If your Sprocker Spaniel drops the bottle initially, just persevere and the length of time your Sprocker Spaniel holds the bottle will improve.

5. You can now start introducing other objects, presenting them with the command 'Grip'. As long as the object is given in the same manner and with the same word of command, it shouldn't be too difficult for your Sprocker Spaniel to grip any object with which you present it.

Chapter Eight: Mission Impossible?

It is true that literally any Sprocker Spaniel can be taught tricks of some kind, but if you have been struggling with yours, there could be a number of factors that are preventing your Sprocker Spaniel from learning any kind of trick. Like within any breed, some are more receptive to learning tricks, while others may be more independent or stubborn.

Stubbornness

It is quite true that some Sprocker Spaniels can simply be stubborn and resist learning tricks. Our 3 puppies were able to learn the basic obedience commands after only a few repetitions, but after showing us that they had learned them, they have steadfastly refused to obey since. If we say 'Come', they will sit down, and if we say 'Sit', they will turn their backs on us. This was never a big issue with us, so we have never bothered again to try to teach them, but those of you with stubborn Sprocker Spaniels will have to work harder to find what motivates your Sprocker Spaniel and use that to teach it tricks.

Impatience

Yes, working with a stubborn Sprocker Spaniel can be frustrating, but dogs in general are very sensitive to our moods and can pick up on negative feelings. Becoming impatient with your Sprocker Spaniel makes it more likely that you will yell at it or even hit it. Keep in mind that when you are training your Sprocker Spaniel, you are also training yourself. Keeping training sessions short will not only keep your Sprocker Spaniel interested, it will also help you remain patient and positive. The owner becoming impatient with the speed at which your Sprocker Spaniel is learning is probably the biggest reason for failure.

Physical Problems

If you have been having trouble teaching your Sprocker Spaniel tricks, the problem might lie in your Sprocker Spaniel's body. Your Sprocker Spaniel just might not be able to jump high, for instance, or it could be that it is harboring some type of longstanding fear.

There could also be a medical reason why your adult or puppy Sprocker Spaniel is not responding as you would wish; Sprocker Spaniels with hip dysplasia will find it impossible to do most tricks. Sprocker Spaniels that have arthritis will also be reluctant to get involved in tricks. If you have any question about your Sprocker Spaniel's physical ability to do tricks, speak to your veterinarian.

Infections can also impact your Sprocker Spaniel's receptivity to instructions, making it less likely to pay attention to you because it is uncomfortable. There could also be hearing issues that are affecting your Sprocker Spaniel's ability to learn tricks – if the latter turns out to be the case, use hand signals.

Mental Slowness

Yes, it's true, some Sprocker Spaniels are just mentally slow. This does not mean that they cannot be taught tricks at all, it does mean that they probably will not be able to learn without very many repetitions, and that you will have to have enormous patience to teach them. You will find geniuses and 'dummies' in every breed, but this will not affect your Sprocker Spaniel's capacity for affection. If you do find that for whatever reason, your Sprocker Spaniel is unable or unwilling to become a star, accept your Sprocker Spaniel as it is, and just enjoy life together.

Chapter Nine: Games for Both of You

If you've been thinking that tricks are a bit one-sided, with your Sprocker Spaniel doing all the activity at your verbal command or physical signal, you'll undoubtedly love to engage in games with your Sprocker Spaniel. Teaching tricks has been a good way for you to work together towards a goal, and will be the foundation of not only doing games together, but also for agility if you are so inclined.

Games will involve activities in which you are both participating, rather than you simply giving commands that your Sprocker Spaniel must obey. When your Sprocker Spaniel is carrying out tricks, it is performing for you, when you are playing games with your Sprocker Spaniel, you are both acting as a team. Some of these games are good for indoors and are great when the weather is so wet, cold, or hot that you don't want to be outside, while others are perfect for the outdoors, and some can be played anywhere.

Also, keep in mind that like any other breed, Sprocker Spaniels need both mental and physical stimulation to stay healthy. Many of the problems that arise with Sprocker Spaniels, such as nuisance barking, aggression, or destructive behavior, come about because your Sprocker Spaniel had no outlet for its energy and simply has become bored. Games with your Sprocker Spaniel will be more fun for both of you if you vary them and keep play sessions fairly short.

As with any activity in which you engage with your Sprocker Spaniel, there are some rules for you to follow in order to have the games safe: try to avoid vigorous outdoor games when the weather is hot. There have been some cases of heat stroke.

Make certain that your adult or puppy Sprocker Spaniel does not have any health problems that could adversely affect it while playing games. Older dogs, too, will probably appreciate shorter, less rigorous game sessions so that they do not get tired out or injure themselves.

Also, if your pup grew up quickly then it should be monitored carefully when engaging in very physical games with them – a fast rate of growth can leave joints somewhat vulnerable to damage.

The Tissue Game

Many years ago, I had a Sprocker Spaniel that was just crazy about this game. We used a piece of ordinary facial tissue, but a small toy or even a little piece of cloth is just as good. This game is played with you sitting in a chair or on the sofa and using the lure to flash between and around your legs. My Sprocker Spaniel would often indicate that she was ready to play the tissue game by coming over and butting her head against my legs. One of the nicest things about the Tissue Game is that there is absolutely no previous training needed for playing it.

1. Wiggle the lure to get your Sprocker Spaniel's attention. If your Sprocker Spaniel doesn't seem to get it, touch your Sprocker Spaniel's nose with the lure and say 'Get it!' in an enthusiastic tone. If tissue is being shredded, or attempted to be eaten by your pooch, use a cloth or a small toy.

2. Move the lure from between the middle of your legs to one side or another and watch your Sprocker Spaniel dart around happily after it. This is a good game for inclement weather days.

Chase

You can make a lure for your Sprocker Spaniel by tying one end of a 2 foot piece of string to a scrap of cloth or a small toy and tying the other end to a stick, or even use a long grass stem with the seed head attached (our puppies just loved this one).

1. After you have prepared the lure, put it on the floor or ground in front of your pup.

2. Wiggle it around a bit to get your Sprocker Spaniel's interest then start pulling it away. Your Sprocker Spaniel's prey drive will probably kick in right away.

3. Most Sprocker Spaniel adults and puppies will start chasing the lure without any encouragement from you.

4. If your Sprocker Spaniel refuses to chase the lure, you can substitute a treat such as a doggie biscuit to challenge their interest.

5. This is a good way to give your Sprocker Spaniel some exercise indoors when the weather is keeping you inside.

Hide and Seek

This game can be played inside or out and makes use not only of your Sprocker Spaniel's desire to be with you, but also of the prey drive that all Sprocker Spaniels possess. If you do play this outside, play it in a fenced yard so that your Sprocker Spaniel doesn't wander off while you're hiding. Most Sprocker Spaniels quickly learn the names of the humans in the household, making your Sprocker Spaniel's participation even easier. Generally speaking, this game is easier with two humans.

1. To begin this game, put your Sprocker Spaniel into 'Stay'.

2. Go to the opposite side of the room and crouch down behind a piece of furniture.

3. Once you are hidden, the human helper should tell your Sprocker Spaniel 'Find Papa (or Mama, or Tommy, or whoever)'.

4. As soon as your Sprocker Spaniel locates the hidden person, give your Sprocker Spaniel a treat and praise it.

5. Your Sprocker Spaniel will probably catch on to how to play this quickly and you can extend the search area to adjoining rooms, or anywhere in the house or yard. You can probably start to give treats only now and again, but keep up with the praise.

Bubbles

This should be done outside unless you want soap residue on your furniture and carpeting. Purchase non-toxic bubble solution so that it won't hurt your Sprocker Spaniel if it does happen to get into its eyes or mouth. In fact, pet stores sell bubble solutions that smell and taste like meat, which should make this game even easier for your Sprocker Spaniel to learn. Start this on a calm day, then wait for a breezy one to really have some fun with your Sprocker Spaniel as it chases after the fleeing bubbles.

1. Sit down so that you are on the same level as your Sprocker Spaniel and call your Sprocker Spaniel to you.

2. When you have your Sprocker Spaniel's attention, blow out a bubble.

3. Curiosity will often spur your Sprocker Spaniel to touch its nose to the bubble.

4. If your Sprocker Spaniel doesn't seem interested, or doesn't seem to know what to do, you can put your own nose near the bubble to give your Sprocker Spaniel the idea.

5. Dogs love to chase things, and most Sprocker Spaniels, once they see a bubble floating past them will go right after it.

Let's Dance!

Your Sprocker Spaniel will have to know how to stand on its hind legs reliably before you can start to teach it to dance. Because this can put a strain on it, make certain that your vet checks out your Sprocker Spaniel, especially the hips and back, before you start teaching your Sprocker Spaniel to trip the light fantastic. When beginning 'Let's Dance', definitely keep the sessions short, particularly if your Sprocker Spaniel hasn't done too much work standing up. Do not try to teach your Sprocker Spaniel to dance unless it has already been through obedience training and at least the intermediate tricks; the more your Sprocker Spaniel is used to working with you, the easier it will be to teach dancing.

1. Tell your Sprocker Spaniel 'Stand Up'. Praise and treat.

2. To get your Sprocker Spaniel to wave its front paws around, hold a treat above its nose. Use a hand signal, such as a waving motion with your right hand to familiarize your Sprocker Spaniel with this phase of the lesson.

3. When you want your Sprocker Spaniel to move towards you on its hind legs, back away from it while holding a treat up above its nose. Make a beckoning motion with your hand now.

4. To get your Sprocker Spaniel to walk backwards, move towards your Sprocker Spaniel, holding the treat above the nose as before. Put your palm towards your Sprocker Spaniel to signal backing up.

5. Always remember to treat and praise at every small positive step.

6. If you want your Sprocker Spaniel to twirl around, circle the treat over your Sprocker Spaniel's head. Make a twirling motion with one hand.

7. Keep practicing with your Sprocker Spaniel these basic steps, adding music to let your Sprocker Spaniel associate the rhythm of the piece you have chosen with its dance movements. Now you can add 'Let's Dance' to your Sprocker Spaniel's vocabulary.

8. As you and your Sprocker Spaniel become more adept as a dance team, you can add some more complicated moves such as

pirouetting under your arm while you hold one of your Sprocker Spaniel's paws, or dipping down then rising up again.

9. Stick to one fairly short musical selection at first and repeat the same steps as you play it; you are actually now the choreographer. Soon your Sprocker Spaniel won't even need hand signals or treats during the performance, but will take its cues from the music and your dance movements.

You can definitely add other pieces of music once your Sprocker Spaniel has learned the first, but be sure that you only add one at a time, and your Sprocker Spaniel should be proficient and confident in each piece before you add another one.

Ball Roll & Toss

This will be best as a game involving 2 people along with your Sprocker Spaniel. Several dogs can also play this as long as you're certain they won't fight. The best kind of ball to use for this is the 'clutch ball' type which is a sculpted ball with indentations that facilitate your Sprocker Spaniel being able to pick up a fairly large ball in its mouth.

1. Position yourself at least 15 feet away from the other person.

2. Show the ball to your Sprocker Spaniel and then toss it to the other person. Hopefully, your Sprocker Spaniel will run in that direction.

3. If your Sprocker Spaniel doesn't seem to catch on, roll the ball, that should definitely get your Sprocker Spaniel's prey drive activated.

4. Once your Sprocker Spaniel starts to play, this can give everyone involved a real workout.

5. When interest begins to flag, let your Sprocker Spaniel 'catch' the ball and chase it to make the end of the game more engaging for your Sprocker Spaniel.

Chapter Ten: Agility – The Ultimate in Games

Have you ever been fascinated watching the talented dogs perform agility feats and wondered whether your Sprocker Spaniel might do well with this? Well, you certainly aren't alone as can be seen by the popularity of agility in so many countries. Considering how many people and dogs are engaged in agility, it might surprise you to learn that it's a relative newcomer on the dog scene.

It all started as a way to keep the audience at the Crufts Dog Show in England from becoming bored while waiting for the next event to start. One of the event organizers, John Varley, can be credited with the idea. Basing the activities of your Sprocker Spaniels on the stunts performed by horses at horse shows, agility was found to be an excellent way to keep the crowd engaged during any hiatus, and it was an instant hit with the audience.

However, the few simple routines initially offered proved to be so overwhelmingly popular that agility now has become one of the favorite activities of dogs and their owners. Shortly after its first introduction, dog owners were demanding classes and events for agility.

It is still a real pleaser when it comes to audiences at dog shows, too, even for those who are not actively engaged in agility with their dog. Agility trials are offered on both an amateur and professional level, and agility can now be considered a very competitive sport. Considering how much a part of your dog world agility now is, it's hard to believe that it only started up in 1978.

Agility is basically an obstacle course laid out for your Sprocker Spaniel to navigate with your assistance. If agility looks like something you might want to become involved in with your Sprocker Spaniel, make sure that your Sprocker Spaniel has 'graduated' from obedience training and is properly socialized.

For those of you who have skipped obedience training, please see our previous book: Sprocker Spaniel Training Guide, for detailed instructions. Likewise, Sprocker Spaniels that have not been socialized will need to be; for those of you who are really becoming involved past the backyard level of agility, it is imperative that your Sprocker Spaniel has the ability to either get along with other dogs or ignore them completely. Any dog acting aggressively towards another at a competition will be eliminated from the trials out of hand.

For those of you who have been teaching tricks and engaging in games with your Sprocker Spaniel, agility could easily be considered the next step up. And, if your Sprocker Spaniel has already been playing with you using a simple obstacle course as mentioned earlier, then the groundwork has already been laid. Clicker training will certainly come in handy here, if you have been training your Sprocker Spaniel with a clicker, but if whatever method you have been using has been successful, then don't hesitate to keep using it – it's never wise to argue with success.

Agility trials will consist of a course that contains between 12 and 18 obstacles. Some of the obstacles, particularly the jumps, will often be repeated over the length of the course. You should keep in mind that there is no set pattern to the obstacles and the set-up will vary from competition to competition.

Prior to beginning the trial, owners and their dogs will have a chance to have a dry run to familiarize themselves with the course, and at this point it's probably better to take your Sprocker Spaniel through it on leash. The differing arrangements at the competitions is why it's a good idea to alter the plan of your own obstacle course from time to time so that your Sprocker Spaniel becomes used to varied course arrangements.

Consider Your Sprocker Spaniel

Theoretically, any Sprocker Spaniel, can participate in agility, but there are still some factors that should be taken into consideration before you begin.

1. The health of your Sprocker Spaniel is the first consideration. Agility is a very demanding sport, and in order for your Sprocker Spaniel to do well in it, and reduce the chance that it will be injured, it should be in top physical condition. A complete checkup at the veterinarian is certainly called for, including blood work. Your Sprocker Spaniel's hips should be free from any degenerative disease or malformation. The spine should be in perfect condition; x-rays can detect any small compression fractures of other problems, and if your Sprocker Spaniel has a family history of hip dysplasia, then additionally have your vet x-ray the hips.

2. The shape and weight of your Sprocker Spaniel will make a difference in how much it is able to accomplish in agility. Heavier Sprocker Spaniels can have a hard time, although there has been success in a variety of cases and so given the correct training and routine, things can work out for you.

3. Make an honest assessment of your Sprocker Spaniel's potential, especially if you are contemplating competitions at a higher level. If you are just going to do agility for fun, then potential will make little or no difference.

4. The age of your Sprocker Spaniel is also important; dogs too young or too old are not good candidates for the intensive demands of agility work. Trials or meets will have age limitations on all dogs.

5. Hyperactive dogs can actually be a good choice for agility. If you have a Sprocker Spaniel that seems to be constantly bouncing off the walls, maybe it's time to channel all that canine energy into something constructive, like agility. Because owners sometimes give up on a hyper dog, you may have to go back and work on obedience first. However, both obedience and agility can provide an outlet for your Sprocker Spaniel's high energy level. With this type of dog, an extra dose of patience on your part will probably be needed, but you may well be surprised at how well your Sprocker Spaniel does do with agility once it gets used to it – and you may have a Sprocker Spaniel that is now calmer and more pleasant to be around. Giving a hyper Sprocker Spaniel something to do is often the best way to cure this problem behavior, and it's certainly better than consigning it to a shelter.

Chapter Eleven: Pre-Agility for Puppies

Important Points

If you think agility looks like something that would be fun for you and your new puppy, there are some things to consider before you leap into the sport.

1. As it is with human children, and with the young of all species with backbones, the growth plates of the bones of puppies are still open. The growth plate is also known as the epiphyseal plate and is responsible for the production of cells that will wind up as actual bone tissue. You can picture your puppy's leg bones as consisting of a middle length of cartilage capped at either end by growth plates. The growth plates are constantly producing new cells which are continuously being pushed toward the center of the leg. As these cells migrate, they begin to ossify, turn to bone, replacing the cartilage. Eventually, the cartilage is all replaced and the place where the cells from both plates finally meet is called the epiphyseal line. Until the growth plates have completed their work, there is always a chance that serious harm could be done to the leg. Puppies that are over-exercised or encouraged to jump or run too much could wind up with damaged, stunted legs and a permanent limp.

2. The joints of puppies can also be damaged by too much physical activity. Between the bones of a dog's joint is cartilage, which provides cushioning so that the bones don't grind together. Jumping too much, and even running too much, can cause the cartilage to become damaged. Arthritis and/or hip dysplasia can result. A limping dog will not be allowed in any agility competition, so go easy on those joints while your Sprocker Spaniel is young.

3. Do not, under any circumstances, use a weighted vest on your Sprocker Spaniel puppy to attempt to build up more muscle; you will only be increasing the probability of damage to the growth plates or joints. These vests could also affect your puppy's balance, making it more likely that the puppy will fall and hurt itself.

4. Avoid using weave poles when starting puppy agility – these can cause torsion, or spiral, fractures to the pup's undeveloped leg bones. A spiral fracture can also occur if the puppy jumps from a high spot. Unlike a 'normal' fracture which is usually a break along the horizontal in the leg, a torsion fracture spirals up the bone. You might consider that in this case the puppy's leg has essentially been twisted apart. Unlike a simple fracture, which is relatively easy to treat, a torsion fracture will require surgery and your vet will probably have to use pins to keep the pieces of the bone together. Most dogs will limp permanently after receiving a spiral fracture, regardless of aftercare.

Easy Does It

If you can't wait to get started on pre-agility training with your Sprocker Spaniel puppy, you should wait until it is at least 4 months old. This is not only a good time for teaching your puppy new skills, but also a window for bonding with you. However, you must keep the activities at a much lower level than you would than if you were working with an adult Sprocker Spaniel.

Keep in mind that reputable agility competitions will not allow a dog to compete until it is 12 months old, and even older for some trials and breeds. Large and giant breed should definitely be kept from performing the higher jumps until they are about 18 months old as their greater weight puts much more stress on the bones and joints that will be experienced by a smaller and lighter puppy.

Never forget that your puppy is just that – a puppy, even when it looks as if it has attained its full growth. Not only will your puppy's attention span be short, but it will also be full of nearly boundless energy, and this is exactly where you will have to exhibit restraint during training; your puppy may want to do more than is good for it. Even if your puppy takes to pre-agility readily and eagerly, you will have to limit training sessions to make sure that too much exercise does not harm the pup.

Pre-agility is a great time to accustom your Sprocker Spaniel puppy to hand signals as well as verbal instruction. Use both when working out with the puppy and you will soon be able to use them interchangeably. Always treat for even the smallest success and completely ignore any slip-up. Never push your puppy to keep trying an obstacle or lesson that is giving problems, this will only activate your puppy's stubborn streak and you will not only find it harder to teach this particular lesson, but others as well. A character in a book once said, "Never give an order unless you're sure it will be obeyed", and these are words of wisdom, even when pertaining to Sprocker Spaniels.

Introducing your Sprocker Spaniel puppy to the basic obstacles of agility at this stage is a good idea as long as you scale the obstacles to your puppy's age and physical condition. Keeping the obstacles as close to the ground as possible will help familiarize your Sprocker Spaniel puppy with them and make it much less likely that an injury will occur. Some people like to enroll their puppies in puppy agility classes, and this can be not only a good idea as far as agility is concerned, but can also help with socialization. One caveat to always keep in mind if you do use a class is to never allow the instructor to have your puppy do something that you think the puppy is unready for, especially anything involving heights. It's your Sprocker Spaniel, after all. Never hesitate to speak up if you disagree with some part of the instruction or if you think the obstacles are too advanced for your puppy. You have hired the instructor, not the other way around.

Interestingly, it's been found that success not only in agility, but in obedience itself, can be linked to whether or not the owner uses puppy or dog training classes. Those who enroll their pups in a class, but only attend one class, have much less success than people who train the puppy or dog entirely by themselves. However, people who join a class with their companion and stick with it, do achieve faster success than those who train their pooch on their own. Evidently, the message here is that if you are going to undertake something, do it completely – either train your Sprocker Spaniel entirely on your own or enroll in a structured class and follow it to the end.

If you decide to work with your Sprocker Spaniel puppy yourself, you can start preparing it for several of the obstacles simply by placing a board on the ground and letting your pup get used to walking, and then running over it. You can keep your puppy on leash to begin with to prevent it darting off the sides, but can eliminate that as soon as the puppy is used to the board and will navigate it without jumping off one side. Staying on the board will be very important when the board has been elevated several feet off the ground. Some pups may be a bit afraid to get on the board right away, but a line of treats leading to the board and continued on the board itself will usually help any puppy get over its fear.

You can start to accustom your Sprocker Spaniel puppy to traveling through the chute by pushing back the fabric nearly to the start and then encouraging your puppy to go through it. As your pup becomes used to the chute, you can add more fabric until the puppy is able to travel through the entire length without problem. Because it's best for your Sprocker Spaniel to go through both the open and collapsed chutes in agility competitions with its nose down, you can help your pup learn this while familiarizing it with the chute.

1. To encourage your Sprocker Spaniel puppy to keep its nose down, tie a small toy or treat to a length of cord and pull it along in front of the puppy. At this point, keep the chute fabric rolls back so you can see what's going on.

2. Keep praising your pup as it runs along the chute in pursuit of the object with its nose down.

3. Alternate using the lure and just encouraging your puppy through the chute using only verbal cues.

4. Add more and more fabric length to the chute as your Sprocker Spaniel puppy becomes more adept at keeping its nose down.

To help your Sprocker Spaniel puppy with the collapsed chute, start by draping a light weight fabric over the end of the open chute – most puppies will have no problem with just plowing through. To simulate the longer collapsed chute, use a bed sheet to gradually add length to the collapsed part of the chute.

As your puppy progresses and grows older and stronger, you can add more challenges to prepare it for actual agility:

1. A tire sitting upright on the ground, through which the puppy can jump.

2. Jumps using both poles and boards can be introduced, but be sure that they are only an inch or two off the ground to start with; you do not want to take a chance with damaging your puppy's bones or joints.

3. Make a 'pseudo' wobble board, only an inch off the ground, to get the puppy used to the uncertain surface. Don't hesitate to keep your hands on your puppy to help it feel confident; don't be surprised if your puppy is skittish at first, this is normal and you should be able to overcome it without too much trouble.

4. Likewise, a teeter-totter that tips only an inch or so to start will accustom the pup to the movement of the board. Use the same technique as detailed above to help your pup overcome any fear it has at the movement of the board. Lead your puppy from one side to the other to help it get accustomed to the jar it will feel when the board hits the ground.

Regardless of whether you are teaching your Sprocker Spaniel puppy pre-agility in your own home and backyard or in a class, always remember to go at your puppy's speed. You want your puppy to feel good about learning these maneuvers and to develop the confidence to continue and do well. Never compare your puppy's progress to another puppy in the class, and try to force your pup to 'catch up'. You're not in a competition at this point, so relax and enjoy working with your puppy, you will get much better and longer lasting results if you proceed at your pup's pace.

If you are starting off with a puppy and have children, why not combine them and get your kids involved in agility. This is not an excuse for you to leave the child and the puppy alone to work on the project, but a way for you, your child, and your puppy to all do this together. Children enjoy doing things with their parents, and this can be a great way not only to introduce your kid to dog agility, but also to impart some important lessons about dog care. Be as patient with your child as you would (or should) be with your puppy. Take it slow and easy so that agility is something both young participants look forward to doing. If your youngster really is enthusiastic about this, you might sign him or her up for junior agility classes. Being around other puppies and dogs will help to get your pup used to different situations and people and can also help with socializing your pup.

Chapter Twelve: Agility Basics for Your Adult Sprocker Spaniel

Now that your puppy has grown up and can be considered to be an adult, it's time to return to the vet for a complete checkup. Explain to your vet that you are interested in agility work with your young adult Sprocker Spaniel and have him or her make sure that your Sprocker Spaniel's hips, legs, and spine are ready to really get going. It's likely that you will get the go-ahead, so you and your Sprocker Spaniel can get down to the fun business of agility. This is also the perfect time to make certain that your Sprocker Spaniel is current on all its shots.

The approach you take to equipment will reflect your agility goals. If you are just planning on doing agility with your Sprocker Spaniel for the fun of it, you can make your own obstacles or use cheaper ones (just make certain they are sturdy enough to prevent injury to your Sprocker Spaniel). However, if you are hoping to take part in judged competitions, you should definitely invest in the highest quality fixtures that you can afford, preferably as close as possible to those that will be used during a competition. This will allow you and your Sprocker Spaniel to become familiar with the obstacles beforehand.

The following are the obstacles used in agility competitions. Your Sprocker Spaniel may already be familiar with these if you have engaged in pre-agility work, but any fit, adult Sprocker Spaniel can also learn how to run the obstacle course as well. If the adult Sprocker Spaniel is coming to these obstacles without any previous experience with them, be sure to introduce your Sprocker Spaniel to them one at a time, and start training slowly. Needless to say, keep a pocketful of treats handy, and do not stint on praise for any small step of progress.

1. Dog Walk. This obstacle is made up of 3 boards, 2 of them being used as ramps and the center one horizontal to the ground. Your Sprocker Spaniel is expected to run up one of the ramps, along the horizontal board, then down the opposite board ramp. The horizontal board is 4 feet above the ground. It should be kept in mind that some sponsoring organizations allow traction slats on the ramp boards, while others do not. Some organizations use rubberized boards for traction. If you are serious about agility, it's probably a good idea to get your Sprocker Spaniel used to boards that provide traction and ones that do not.

2. A-Frame. The A-Frame is an obstacle that requires your Sprocker Spaniel to climb up one fairly steep ramp, then scramble down the other side on an equally steep ramp. Each ramp is between 8 to 9 feet in length and 3 feet in breadth. The ramps are connected at the top with a hinge. As with the Dog Walk, some organizations allow the use of slats on the ramps to provide footing for your Sprocker Spaniels. Be aware that some competitions will not allow the use of slatted ramps, however. Rubberized A-Frame ramps are allowed, also.

3. Pause Table. This is, as it says, a 'table' onto which your Sprocker Spaniel must jump and then either sit or lie for a designated period of time – generally only about 5 seconds. The table is 3 feet square, but can be set at different heights. Some Pause Tables are only 8 inches high, while others are over 2 feet in height (the height will be determined by the height of your Sprocker Spaniel). Besides the Pause Table, some trials will have what is called a Pause Box. This is simply an area on the ground demarcated by tape or perhaps sections of PVC pipe laid on the ground. It would be a good idea to get your Sprocker Spaniel used to this, and use the same command for the Pause Box and you would for the Pause Table. Remember, the simpler you make things, the greater the chance for success at a trial.

4. Teeter-Totter. Based on the children's toy, this is one of the most challenging of obstacles to teach to a Sprocker Spaniel. The abrupt slamming down of the board as your Sprocker Spaniel travels across the midpoint is frightening to most Sprocker Spaniels, at least initially. The midpoint of the Teeter-Totter is several feet above the ground, and one side of the 12 foot board is slightly longer than the other so that the board always descends on that side when not in use. There are no slats or other traction elements on the Teeter-Totter. As can be expected, your Sprocker Spaniel runs up the side of the board on the ground, reaches midpoint, then descends as its weight forces the other side down.

5. Tunnel. Made of what is, in effect, a long wire spiral covered with vinyl, and is 10 to 20 feet long. Because of the flexibility of the wire spiral, the tunnel can be straight or positioned into curves. In order to keep the tunnel from moving while your Sprocker Spaniel is traversing it, sandbags are often used to provide stability.

6. Collapsed Tunnel. Unlike the regular Tunnel, the Collapsed Tunnel consists of a short stationery arch or a cylinder with a tube of fabric fastened to it, which lies flat on the ground. Your Sprocker Spaniel enters through the arch and must then make its way through the fabric to come out of the other end.

7. Basic Jump. Also called the Hurdle, the Basic Jump consists of an obstacle with a horizontal bar that can be adjusted to the height of your Sprocker Spaniel. The bar is supported in place by vertical stanchions. Some jumps have 'wings' to either side of the jump itself, which serve mostly to keep the handler from getting too close to your Sprocker Spaniel as it goes over the jump.

8. Panel Jump. Rather than use bars or poles, this jump uses a solid board instead. As with the Basic Jump, the height of your Sprocker Spaniel will determine the height of the jump.

9. Spread Jump. In this jump, which uses horizontal bars, the bars are all aligned on the different levels, and separated from one another to cause your Sprocker Spaniel to traverse not only a vertical plane, but also a horizontal one. The amount of spread, as well as the height, will depend upon the size of your Sprocker Spaniel.

10. Tire Jump. Whether an actual tire is used, which has been carefully wrapped with tape to prevent your Sprocker Spaniels' feet from becoming entangled, or a specially designed 'tire', the effect is the same – your Sprocker Spaniel will have to jump through the tire. Suspended in a frame, the height of the tire will be adjusted to fit your Sprocker Spaniel.

11. Broad Jump. This obstacle will test your Sprocker Spaniel's ability to jump over several panels which have been laid out on the ground. While the panels are only inches above the ground, the width of the jump can vary according to your Sprocker Spaniel.

12. Weave Poles. All of us have seen videos of dogs snapping through Weave Poles at agility competitions. The poles are 2 feet apart, and depending on the competition, there will be between 6 and 12 poles. Weave Poles are the most challenging of obstacles. Your Sprocker Spaniel must begin its run through the poles on the right side and has to go around every one in sequence. Because of the strain Weave Poles can put upon a dog's body, take this obstacle slowly when training your Sprocker Spaniel, and once again, make sure your Sprocker Spaniel's body is fully mature to help prevent fractures and other injuries.

Chapter Thirteen: Getting Your Sprocker Spaniel Started

Now that you understand what kinds of obstacles agility competitions will contain, and you have supplied yourself with the proper equipment, it's time to get started on training your Sprocker Spaniel (and yourself). Once again, if you haven't taught obedience to your Sprocker Spaniel yet, you absolutely must go back and train your Sprocker Spaniel adequately; a Sprocker Spaniel with no obedience training will simply be unable to master agility in a reasonable amount of time.

Your Sprocker Spaniel must also be able to respond positively to your commands when it is off leash – no leashes are allowed in agility, your Sprocker Spaniel will be reacting to your verbal and physical cues. If you have been teaching your Sprocker Spaniel tricks, you'll find that many of these will make teaching agility that much easier; if your Sprocker Spaniel already knows 'Jump', then transferring this to the different jumps required during an agility competition will be a snap.

As with puppies, Sprocker Spaniel adults will do better with the obstacles if they are introduced to them gradually. Get your Sprocker Spaniel used to walking on boards while they are still on the ground. If your Sprocker Spaniel slips off or jumps off, no harm will come to it at this point. Introduce your Sprocker Spaniel to one obstacle at a time, and only progress to the next once your Sprocker Spaniel is comfortable with the first.

When training for obstacles like your Dog Walk, raise the board incrementally off the ground until it is at the regulation height. This will help your Sprocker Spaniel develop balance as the board gets higher and higher off the ground and help prevent acrophobia.

In addition to introducing your Sprocker Spaniel to the obstacles, it will also have to learn a new set of commands in order to successfully complete an agility course. It probably won't take as long for your Sprocker Spaniel to learn these as it was to learn commands initially since your Sprocker Spaniel is already used to responding to your directives.

1. Move. There is a time limitation to all competitive agility meets and regardless of how effectively your Sprocker Spaniel goes through the obstacles, they will either lose points or be disqualified if they are too slow. 'Move' is designed to give your Sprocker Spaniel a mental push to get it to run faster. Put your Sprocker Spaniel on leash and start out walking, speed up to a trot and say 'Move'. Progress to a run while giving the command.

2. Go. This cue will indicate to your Sprocker Spaniel which obstacle it must go to next. There is no set designation for obstacles at any agility competition; the obstacles can be arranged any way the organizers see fit. You can teach this either with a treat or a toy. Put your Sprocker Spaniel into a 'Stay', hold onto its collar, and then toss the treat or toy several feet away. Release your Sprocker Spaniel and say 'Go'. When you tell your Sprocker Spaniel 'Go' also point at the toy or treat, to accustom your Sprocker Spaniel to hand signals.

3. Up. You will need this cue for your Dog Walk and A-Frame. This cue will be especially easy to teach if you already allow your Sprocker Spaniel onto the furniture. Every time you see your Sprocker Spaniel heading towards the couch or an armchair, as soon as it starts to jump, say 'Up'. You can also pat the furniture to draw your Sprocker Spaniel's interest. If your Sprocker Spaniel has been forbidden the furniture, you can substitute a box or a rock outside. Pat the box or rock and say 'Up'. If your Sprocker Spaniel doesn't jump up on its own, lift your Sprocker Spaniel onto the object, saying 'Up' as you do so.

4. Through. You will need to teach this command mostly for the tunnels, but it can also be useful for the jumping obstacles. (If your Sprocker Spaniel is already an ace at 'Jump' just stick to this command for the jumps.) You can make a short tunnel out of kitchen chairs and a sheet to get your Sprocker Spaniel used to the idea, or simply use an agility tunnel that has been compressed somewhat so that your Sprocker Spaniel can easily see the end. A helper can hold your Sprocker Spaniel at the opposite end while you wait with a treat at the other. Tell your Sprocker Spaniel 'Through' and wave the treat around so it can see it.

5. Tunnel. As your Sprocker Spaniel becomes familiar with the 'Through' command, it's time to help it identify the obstacle that it will be used for. Once your Sprocker Spaniel is reliably going through your tunnel on cue, start saying 'Tunnel' or 'Through Tunnel'. Linking the word 'tunnel' with the 'Through' command will make it easier for your Sprocker Spaniel to understand what you want.

6. Cross. Because you and your Sprocker Spaniel will be darting all over the obstacle course during a competition, there will be times when your Sprocker Spaniel will have to cross in front of you to reach the next challenge. This works best with a helper. Tell your Sprocker Spaniel 'Stay' and have your helper hold your Sprocker Spaniel to your left. Throw a treat or toy to your right and have the helper let go of your Sprocker Spaniel as you say 'Cross'. Make sure you practice both right and left crosses.

7. Weave. Your 'Weave' command will let your Sprocker Spaniel know that it's time to go through the weave poles. The weave poles are probably the place where most dogs 'wash out' during a competition so make certain that your Sprocker Spaniel not only knows the 'Weave' command but will also respond to it quickly.

8. Plank. Your Sprocker Spaniel will have to navigate several obstacles that involve planks or boards, as we have detailed

previously. Using one command for the A-Frame, Teeter-Totter, and Dog Walk can help simplify the process for your Sprocker Spaniel and make it more likely that it will act quickly on your command.

9. Slow. This command would prove to be useful if your Sprocker Spaniel may be taking some of the obstacles too enthusiastically, such as your Dog Walk. When the possibility of an injury exists because your Sprocker Spaniel is going too fast, teaching it the 'Slow' command is important. You can do this by trotting with your Sprocker Spaniel on leash, then slowing down to a walk and saying 'Slow'.

10. Jump. Since your Sprocker Spaniel probably already understands this command, it should be easy to transfer it from tricks to agility. Run your Sprocker Spaniel up to one of the jump obstacles, say 'Jump' and more than likely your Sprocker Spaniel will sail right over it. Don't make the jumps too high to begin with and always scale them to the height of your Sprocker Spaniel.

11. Chute. This command can be used when your Sprocker Spaniel will be going through the collapsed tunnel, or you can just use the 'Tunnel' command when approaching it. If your Sprocker Spaniel is really quick to respond to learning new commands, then you can certainly add 'Chute', but if 'Tunnel' works just as well, stick with that.

12. Tire. One of the obstacles at an agility meet is a tire suspended within a framework. While the jump command could be used when running to the tire, giving the specific cue 'Tire' can help your Sprocker Spaniel focus on the target and could prevent confusion.

13. Table. Use 'Table' to get your Sprocker Spaniel onto the Pause Table, which will also involve sitting or lying down on it for approximately 5 seconds.

Once again, it cannot be stressed more that patience and positive reinforcement are the real keys to successful agility. Your Sprocker Spaniel is not trying to defy you when it doesn't comprehend what you want it to do, it just needs more time to learn. Any time you feel yourself becoming frustrated and angry is the time to stop the agility lessons. A dog that fears punishment, even if it's just a tongue lashing, will learn at a much slower rate just because its mind is on avoiding punishment, rather than the task at hand.

Take the lessons as slowly as your Sprocker Spaniel needs. Some Sprocker Spaniels will catch on almost immediately. However, nearly every Sprocker Spaniel that is physically able can become a star in its own way in agility. You may not have a Sprocker Spaniel that will be a competitor in agility trials, but you will have a Sprocker Spaniel that is having fun doing something with the person it loves most – you – and that is every bit as important as having a Sprocker Spaniel that wins blue ribbons.

If you have been using a clicker for training tricks and games, then continue to use it for agility. Also keep plenty of treats on hand; there are delicious, low calorie treats such as freeze-dried liver chunks that dogs love, and they won't add to your Sprocker Spaniel's waistline. Breaking up the training sessions with a bit of play also helps your Sprocker Spaniel learn agility more quickly and makes it more pleasant for both of you.

Another thing that can make a world of difference in agility trials is where you will be during the run. It's a good idea to decide now where you will be holding yourself in relation to your Sprocker Spaniel – will you have your Sprocker Spaniel on your left or on your right side? Choosing a side that is comfortable for you and sticking with it right from the start will help both of you navigate the obstacle course much more easily. The decision can be made simply on the basis of whether you are right- or left-handed.

Although you will not be able to use them in competitions, there are a few more items that can help to make agility training easier:

1. Targeting sticks are simply lightweight sticks about 3 feet long that you use to point out where you want your Sprocker Spaniel to go and say 'Table' for instance. Dogs tend to follow the direction in which you point naturally, so this can help your Sprocker Spaniel understand your directions more easily.

2. Targeting discs can also help your Sprocker Spaniel find its way through an agility course. Use a premade disc or simply use an old lid from a food container. Toss the disc where you want your Sprocker Spaniel to go, at the same time naming the obstacle.

3. Many people find that using a leash to help their dog through the obstacle course can make the learning process go faster initially. A leash will also keep your Sprocker Spaniel from taking off on its own once it's tired of the lessons or when something has drawn its attention. Don't reprimand your Sprocker Spaniel in this case, either. If your Sprocker Spaniel is getting bored, continuing will be counterproductive. If your Sprocker Spaniel wants to chase the neighbor's cat, simply hold it by your side until it calms down and try going through the lesson again.

4. Keep attuned to your Sprocker Spaniel's attitude. Not only should you be alert for signs of boredom, but also for signs of stress. If your Sprocker Spaniel is laying back its ears or starting to tuck its tail, it's time to stop. Nervous head gestures or moving indecisively are also indicators that lessons are over. Your Sprocker Spaniel will learn much more quickly when it's relaxed and comfortable.

Starting with Jumps

Jumps are a good place to start when you begin agility training, there are numerous jumps on every agility field. We already covered the different kinds of jumps your Sprocker Spaniel can expect to find during a meet, so it's a good idea to set up a variety of jumps when you begin to train your Sprocker Spaniel.

Start with the jump at the lowest level, regardless of your Sprocker Spaniel's ability, to accustom your Sprocker Spaniel to it before raising higher. Don't overdo jump practice as it can increase the possibility of your Sprocker Spaniel becoming injured. Keep the sessions short to begin with to give your Sprocker Spaniel's body time to adjust to jumping.

1. Walk your Sprocker Spaniel through a short course of single jumps, giving the command 'Jump' as you approach the obstacle. If you are using a leash, abandon it as soon as possible; you will not be allowed to use a leash at a trial.

2. Once your Sprocker Spaniel is familiar with this, start going through the course at a trot. At this point you should not be using a leash at all, if you still find it necessary, go back to walking your Sprocker Spaniel through your course.

3. Raise the height of the jumps gradually as your Sprocker Spaniel becomes used to them.

4. Add in the broad jump and plank jump as your Sprocker Spaniel progresses.

Getting Used to the Tire

Because the tire jump is just another jump, it's best to add this now to your Sprocker Spaniel's training. Let the base of the tire rest on the ground to start.

1. Lead your Sprocker Spaniel up to the tire and say either 'Jump' or 'Tire', whichever command you have decided to use. Don't interchange the terms, choose one and stick with it.

2. As with the other jumps, walk your Sprocker Spaniel through it to begin with.

3. When your Sprocker Spaniel is reliably going through the tire from a walk, advance to a trot and then a run. (Some enthusiastic Sprocker Spaniels will want to take the tire jump at a run right from the start.)

4. Gradually raise the tire until it's at the correct height for your Sprocker Spaniel in competition.

5. Use tape to wrap the tire so that your Sprocker Spaniel's feet don't get caught when it's going through.

Dog Walk

There will definitely be a Dog Walk at every agility trial, so getting your Sprocker Spaniel used to this is absolutely essential. Using the command 'Up' will help to keep the instruction clear in your Sprocker Spaniel's mind, and using only one word will allow it to focus better. The three boards should be hinged so that there is no chance of them sliding out of place. It would probably be a good idea to teach your Sprocker Spaniel to use both slatted and smooth boards as either may be offered.

1. Lay the boards that will be used in your Dog Walk on the ground. The middle board can simply be flat at this time.

2. Lead your Sprocker Spaniel to one end of your Dog Walk and say 'Up' as you lead your Sprocker Spaniel onto the board.

3. Some Sprocker Spaniels may be afraid to step onto the boards, but you can overcome this by placing a line of treats on the board, or placing your Sprocker Spaniel partway down one of the boards. Hold your Sprocker Spaniel's leash so that it can't just step off. If your Sprocker Spaniel starts to back up to get off the board, let it, this will help it accustom itself to the board, too.

4. Once your Sprocker Spaniel is comfortable walking over the boards when they are resting on the ground, you can start to raise the middle one. Do this incrementally, and make sure that your Dog Walk is absolutely stable.

5. Let your Sprocker Spaniel walk over your Dog Walk once it has been raised to the regulation height of 4 feet, then gradually increase the pace. Keep your Sprocker Spaniel on leash as you proceed to trot and run to help stabilize it.

6. As soon as your Sprocker Spaniel is able to navigate your Dog Walk at a run without problems while on leash, you can take the leash off. If your Sprocker Spaniel slows down initially when off leash on your Dog Walk, just give it time to gain confidence.

7. Don't hesitate to retrace steps if your Sprocker Spaniel is having problems; it's better to handle any problems slowly than to push your Sprocker Spaniel.

A-Frame

Because the A-Frame is another elevated obstacle that could potentially cause harm were your Sprocker Spaniel to fall from it, you should also take this one slowly. This is one of the more difficult obstacles for your Sprocker Spaniel to master, but any agile Sprocker Spaniel should be able to learn how to do it successfully. You will be using the command 'Up' again. Remember that you will be doing more pointing than speaking during a trial, so always combine your verbal command with the physical indication.

The A-Frame is relatively steep, so once again, begin with the obstacle flat or nearly flat on the ground. This will also help your Sprocker Spaniel get used to the slats that it will use for traction once the A-Frame is elevated. Always remember to make sure that at whatever the elevation of the A-Frame that it has been completely stabilized.

1. If your Sprocker Spaniel has already been working on your Dog Walk, it will probably not balk at walking over the A-Frame. You can even begin with the obstacle raised a few inches in the middle off the ground.

2. As your Sprocker Spaniel becomes more familiar with the A-Frame, gradually raise the center until it has reached the maximum height of 5′ 6″.

3. Train your Sprocker Spaniel to keep to the center of the A-Frame as much as possible to prevent it falling off while on the obstacle.

4. By starting the A-Frame at a very low level, you will help build up your Sprocker Spaniel's muscles to deal with what is actually climbing, as well as learning how to navigate the down side of the obstacle without losing its balance.

Tunnel

Teaching your Sprocker Spaniel to navigate the tunnel is not as difficult as you may think, especially if you have the assistance of a helper. Tunnels can vary between 10 and 20 feet.

1. Reduce the length of the tunnel as much as possible so that your Sprocker Spaniel can easily see the far end.

2. Have your helper hold your Sprocker Spaniel at one end of the tunnel while you squat near the other end.

3. Call your Sprocker Spaniel and hold out a treat, while giving the command 'Tunnel'. Your Sprocker Spaniel will most likely come right through the tunnel to you. If your Sprocker Spaniel hesitates, throw the treat about halfway down the tunnel to encourage your Sprocker Spaniel.

4. Once your Sprocker Spaniel is comfortable negotiating the short tunnel, lengthen it out, and when it will go through the longer tunnel confidently you can start adding curves.

5. Secure the tunnel in some way to make sure it doesn't roll while your Sprocker Spaniel is in it. This is ordinarily done with sandbags, but braces are also available that will hold the tunnel still.

Chute

Whether you use the cue 'Chute' or 'Tunnel' for this obstacle is up to you, just make certain that you choose one and stick with it.

1. If your Sprocker Spaniel is already familiar with the tunnel, it will probably be easier for it to learn how to go through the chute.

2. Use a helper to hold your Sprocker Spaniel at the open end while you station yourself at the collapsed fabric.

3. Because your Sprocker Spaniel will not realize that it can go through the fabric, in most cases, hold the cloth so that the end of the chute is only partially covered. Make sure that your Sprocker Spaniel can see you.

4. Call your Sprocker Spaniel with a 'Come' and as soon as it's released and making its way towards you, say 'Tunnel' (or 'Chute').

5. Lower the level of the fabric as the lesson is repeated, and finally leave the tunnel totally collapsed on the fabric end.

6. Lead your Sprocker Spaniel up to the open end at a run, give the command signal and your Sprocker Spaniel will probably run right through without problem.

Pause Table

Because they are so enthused about going through the course, many dogs get caught up on the Pause Table. After running fully out, your Sprocker Spaniel will be expected to jump onto the Pause Table, sit or lie down, and wait until given the cue to continue. This, of course, will really test a dog's training and self-control, but with practice, your Sprocker Spaniel will master the Pause Table, too.

1. Pat the table, say 'Table' to encourage your Sprocker Spaniel to get onto it. If your Sprocker Spaniel doesn't seem to understand,

place a treat on the table and repeat until your Sprocker Spaniel will jump onto the table without problem.

2. When your Sprocker Spaniel is on the table say either 'Down' or 'Sit'. Your Sprocker Spaniel should comply with your command. Decide on one term to use and stay with it, going back and forth can confuse your Sprocker Spaniel and make it more likely that it will fail this part of the trial. In general, your Sprocker Spaniel will have to remain on the Pause Table from 5 to 10 seconds.

3. As your Sprocker Spaniel begins to respond better to its instructions and will reliably jump onto the table then become stationary, you will have to get it moving again. Use the 'Go' command to get your Sprocker Spaniel going and run along with it to give it the right idea.

Teeter-Totter

This can be one of the more difficult of the obstacles for your Sprocker Spaniel to get used to. The abrupt slamming motion when your pooch crosses the midpoint of the Teeter-Totter is off-putting to a lot of dogs. Because this obstacle can startle your Sprocker Spaniel, you may have to take this one very slowly and use plenty of treats. As there is always the danger of your Sprocker Spaniel falling off the Teeter-Totter, especially when moving at speed, it's vital that you help your Sprocker Spaniel develop the balance and confidence when dealing with this obstacle. To begin with, use a leash with your Sprocker Spaniel. You will be using the 'Go' command with this obstacle while pointing at it.

1. As you did with your Dog Walk and A-Frame, start off with your 'Teeter-Totter' nearly flat on the floor. Place a dowel under a board to serve as the fulcrum. Position the dowel so that the side your Sprocker Spaniel will be walking up on will already be on the floor or ground. Point to the board and say 'Go'.

2. Lead your Sprocker Spaniel on leash towards the fulcrum and let it step so that the board lowers in the direction your Sprocker Spaniel is facing.

3. Don't be surprised if your Sprocker Spaniel is startled to begin with, even with a relatively small drop, but the leash should prevent your Sprocker Spaniel leaving the board.

4. When your Sprocker Spaniel seems comfortable navigating the entire length of the Teeter-Totter, use a larger fulcrum. You can keep increasing the size, but always keep in mind that the Teeter-Totter must be absolutely stable to prevent accidents. If you make your own obstacle, make sure that it won't tip your Sprocker Spaniel off or collapse when your Sprocker Spaniel uses it. At this point, keep your Sprocker Spaniel on leash – this will not only serve to control your Sprocker Spaniel, but to make it feel more confident.

5. As you raise the height of the Teeter-Totter, watch to see whether your Sprocker Spaniel becomes startled at the sound when the board smacks down onto the floor. Keep an eye on your Sprocker Spaniel when this happens at first to make sure it doesn't try to bolt off the board to the side.

6. Once your Sprocker Spaniel can go from one side of the Teeter-Totter without problem on the leash, it's time to remove the leash. Point to the obstacle and say 'Go'.

7. To get your Sprocker Spaniel to speed things up on the Teeter-Totter, add the 'Move' command.

8. Some Sprocker Spaniels will be afraid of the Teeter-Totter regardless of how you have tried to train them. The problem here is usually that your Sprocker Spaniel is fearful of being on what seems to be an unsteady surface. The answer to this is a wobble board. Use a small object under a piece of plywood that is large enough to accommodate your Sprocker Spaniel comfortably. A small object to start will allow the wobble board to move around,

but not enough to alarm your Sprocker Spaniel. Increasing the size of the object as your Sprocker Spaniel develops its balance will help prepare it for the challenge of the Teeter-Totter.

Weave Poles

Weave Poles are probably the most difficult of the agility obstacles to teach to your Sprocker Spaniel. Remember, however, that thousands and thousands of dogs have been able to master this obstacle successfully, thanks to patience, positive reinforcement, and dedication on the part of their owners. You will achieve success more quickly when teaching the Weave Poles to your Sprocker Spaniel if you use a helper to begin with. It's probably best to use 'Weave' to get your Sprocker Spaniel going on this obstacle; this will help to distinguish it from the other obstacles and help your Sprocker Spaniel to focus on the poles. The point is to make it as simple as possible for your Sprocker Spaniel to navigate the obstacle course.

Remember, the Weave Poles should not be a part of your Sprocker Spaniel's repertoire until it is fully adult and the growth plates in the bones have fused. Permanent damage can be done to your Sprocker Spaniel's legs if you try to start teaching this obstacle while your Sprocker Spaniel is still a puppy. Keep in mind that limping dogs are not allowed to enter any agility competition.

1. Begin to teach the Weave Poles by spreading the poles apart to the sides so that your Sprocker Spaniel can simply walk through them as if it was walking between two walls. This will allow your Sprocker Spaniel to become familiar with the poles without actually having to twist and turn.

2. Your helper should hold onto your Sprocker Spaniel at one end of the Weave Poles while you walk through them.

3. Once you reach the far end of the Weave Poles, call your Sprocker Spaniel as your helper releases it.

4. As soon as your Sprocker Spaniel will come to you without hesitation, you can dispense with your human helper.

5. Place your Sprocker Spaniel in a 'Sit' and 'Stay' at one end of the spread poles. Go to the opposite end and pat your legs and use your chosen command word now. There should be no problem with your Sprocker Spaniel coming right to you.

6. As soon as your Sprocker Spaniel does this without problem, it's time to change the game a bit: after putting your Sprocker Spaniel in a 'Stay', walk on the outside of the spread poles and then call your Sprocker Spaniel. If your Sprocker Spaniel strays outside the poles, perhaps trying to follow in your footsteps, use a leash to lead it through the poles while you continue to walk on the outside.

7. Now it's time to start moving the poles closer together. Do this in small increments to make it easier for your Sprocker Spaniel. Make sure that you have set up the poles so that your Sprocker Spaniel enters them on the right side – conditioning your Sprocker Spaniel to feel the touch of the pole on its left shoulder will help teach your Sprocker Spaniel the right way to begin the Weave Poles.

8. You may have to use a leash once the poles begin to tighten up, and don't hesitate to use treats as well to help your Sprocker Spaniel understand what is required. Once again, yelling or other signs of impatience are not only unnecessary, but counterproductive.

9. Don't wait until the weave poles have been placed in their correct position before you and your Sprocker Spaniel begin to take them at a run. Getting your Sprocker Spaniel to run through the poles while they are still some distance apart will make it easier and help to develop your Sprocker Spaniel's balance further.

10. Remember to begin every run with your target command word, 'Weave', and by pointing. Always make certain that your Sprocker Spaniel is beginning on the right side of the poles.

11. Should your Sprocker Spaniel be having difficulty in keeping on course after the poles have been put into a straight line, you can use guides to help keep your Sprocker Spaniel on course. These are flexible attachments for the poles that not only prevent your Sprocker Spaniel from leaving the obstacle, but that also keep your Sprocker Spaniel close to the poles.

12. If your Sprocker Spaniel is having trouble getting through 12 or 18 poles, why not start with a fewer number? Getting your Sprocker Spaniel to go through 4 or 6 poles successfully, then gradually working up the number can make it a lot easier for a dog that may be having difficulty. Don't hesitate to use the leash to guide your Sprocker Spaniel if it's having trouble.

Putting It All Together

Once your Sprocker Spaniel has learned each obstacle and will perform as required with only the command word and your hand signal, it's time to begin putting together an obstacle course to provide practice runs for you and your Sprocker Spaniel. Always keep in mind that there is no 'set in stone' way that agility courses will be set up at trials, it is always at the discretion of the trial organizers. For this reason, it's a good idea to vary your course to accustom your Sprocker Spaniel to the vagaries of any particular meet.

If you haven't spent as much time as you should have in using hand signals, now is the time to conduct a crash course. You will need to rely on signaling your Sprocker Spaniel this way during a trial because in most cases, your Sprocker Spaniel will be outrunning you. To do this successfully, set up only a few obstacles at your home course and use only your hand and body language to get your Sprocker Spaniel to move.

Be patient if this is fairly new to your Sprocker Spaniel, but if you run along with your Sprocker Spaniel and use only hand signals to direct your Sprocker Spaniel, it should catch on quickly. Change the course around as you work on this and add more obstacles to familiarize your Sprocker Spaniel more thoroughly. And when you do use verbal commands, make sure that you 'bark' them out loudly and enthusiastically.

Call-Offs

It's probably inevitable that at some time during either training, or during a trial, that your Sprocker Spaniel will start to go to the wrong obstacle. As this can be an instant elimination in a trial, it's important that you teach your Sprocker Spaniel a command or two to direct it. You can simply use 'Here' and point to show your Sprocker Spaniel the correct route. You can teach this command by using the word and pointing where you want your Sprocker Spaniel to go. By this time, your Sprocker Spaniel has already learned so many commands that it should be easier for it to learn another one.

To further refine the call-off you can use the commands 'Go Right' and 'Go Left'. Teaching these commands will be especially important not only in reference to the Weave Poles, but also when your Sprocker Spaniel is at risk of taking the wrong direction after completing an obstacle. Most dogs will simply want to continue in a straight line towards the next obstacle, but if the next one in the course is to one side, or even out of your Sprocker Spaniel's line of sight, these directional commands can get your Sprocker Spaniel moving the right way.

There can be as many as 20 obstacles at an agility trial, so it's important for you to be in good physical condition, too, as you will have to run along with your Sprocker Spaniel. If you're a bit out of shape, this is the perfect time to condition yourself as well as help your Sprocker Spaniel prepare for an agility trial. Make sure that the clothes you choose are comfortable and will allow you freedom of movement. Your shoes should be lightweight, but provide good traction. If you have long hair, you may want to tie it back while running a course.

1. Begin by putting 2 or 3 of the obstacles in a line. A jump on either side of your Dog Walk is a good way to start.

2. Start to run with your Sprocker Spaniel, point at the first jump, and say 'Jump'.

3. As you approach your Dog Walk, give the 'Up' command and point as you run alongside.

4. Finish up with a 'Jump' at the last jump and then treat and praise your Sprocker Spaniel.

5. You can keep adding obstacles, but it's also a good idea to research online (and offline) for places that provide maps of 'official' obstacle courses at agility trials.

6. In order to help prepare your Sprocker Spaniel for a successful trial, change the order of the obstacles around – there is no 'set' pattern for agility trials.

Hopefully, everything has gone well for you and no insurmountable problems have arisen. However, it would be naïve to assume that every Sprocker Spaniel takes to agility smoothly; in fact the opposite is probably true in more cases than not. Should you find yourself having problems with agility training, don't hesitate to seek out the services of a professional trainer. Don't just drop your Sprocker Spaniel off, either, stay with it so that you can learn how to train and support it. Obviously, it's perfectly possible to teach your Sprocker Spaniel agility on your own, and many people consider this to be the best way to do so, but if you are having some problems or simply don't have enough time, don't hesitate to enroll your Sprocker Spaniel with a trainer.

Although there are a few organizations that offer cash prizes for success in agility trials, most do not, but few people participate in agility with their dogs for financial gain, they are simply competing for fun. Accumulating ribbons, medals, and trophies, however, shows how well you and your Sprocker Spaniel are doing in this sport.

Chapter Fourteen: Getting Involved in Agility

Once you have done all you can to train your Sprocker Spaniel in agility (or participated in trainer-run agility classes), you might feel that it's time to get actively involved. There are actually two ways to start agility competitions: matches and trials. Regardless of how well you and your Sprocker Spaniel have performed to date, it's probably a good idea to start with matches.

Agility Matches

If you have not yet joined a local agility club, this is probably an excellent time to do so. Local agility clubs will generally allow puppies as young as 4 months old (just when you would be starting training) to participate in matches. If you do start with a local club when your Sprocker Spaniel is a puppy, it will not only learn agility safely, but will also have a great chance to become socialized with the other pets there. The puppy will also become accustomed to being around larger numbers of people, reducing the chance of nervousness during a trial.

Another plus to matches is that they are open not only to pure-breed dogs, but also to mixed-breeds, which are denied participation in many competitive trials. Mixed breed dogs can be every bit as good at agility as pure-breed dogs, so this will give your favorite 'mutt' a chance to shine too.

Keep in mind, however, that your work in matches will not be used as any kind of official recognition with regards to competitive trials. There are no certificates or ribbons given at matches that will increase your standing at any trial, but matches are still an excellent way to practice, help your Sprocker Spaniel adult or puppy become socialized, and meet new people. There is much less pressure at matches, with the emphasis being on having fun. Many people never go any further than matches.

Competitive Trials

If you have joined a local agility club and you and your Sprocker Spaniel have done well at matches, you may well consider moving on to competitive trials. Trials have a much more structured format than do matches. Dogs younger than 12 months, or in some cases 18 months, will not be allowed in them as they are much more rigorous than matches.

Also unlike matches, if you want to participate in a trial you will have to register well in advance. You will then receive a list of trials that will be available, and depending on your financial situation (there are fees associated with Competitive Trials as well as any possible travel costs) and available time, you will be able to arrange a trial schedule for you and your Sprocker Spaniel. In order for your Sprocker Spaniel's agility trials to 'count' as far as progression in the sport goes, you will need to enroll in trials that are run by certain agility clubs. For those in the United States, the American Kennel Club (AKC) is a good place to start for trial information. If you live in the United Kingdom, the United Kennel Club (UKC) sponsors trials.

Junior Class Agility

Kids and dogs are naturals together, and one of the best ways to learn agility with your Sprocker Spaniel is to start out young. The AKC sponsors classes and events for children and their dogs not only to keep interest alive in agility, but also to help children learn the proper way to train their dogs. These classes are also a great way for kids to learn the principles of sportsmanship. The classes offered are called AKC Junior Showmanship Classes and they are divided into 3 categories:

1. The Junior Class is for children who are no younger than 9 years old, but not yet 12.

2. The Intermediate Class is designed for kids between the ages of 12 and 14.

3. The Senior Class is for youths who are 15 years old, but have not yet turned 18.

The division of classes by age group will help less experienced children gain confidence in handling their Sprocker Spaniel during an agility trial. There are some regulations that must be met: your Sprocker Spaniel being presented by the child must either be the child's dog or the family dog; your Sprocker Spaniel has to meet the age requirements; children and their dogs must dress and behave appropriately. Most local dog clubs will offer junior memberships. It's often a good idea for youngsters interested in dog agility to attend some Junior Class Agility shows; this will give them a chance to see firsthand how a trial is conducted and also get acquainted with children who are already active in agility.

Other agility clubs for children and teens will have different requirements, with some children as young as 5 being permitted to join. Most agility clubs will provide training classes.

Chapter Fifteen: The Agility Trial

The Rules

Perhaps before you begin actively training your Sprocker Spaniel in agility, you should familiarize yourself with exactly what is required at an agility meet. This can help to avoid disappointment and frustration. As stated before, the obstacle course arrangement will vary from trial to trial, although all of the obstacles will be used. There are a few general rules that will apply at every agility trial:

1. No food or treats are allowed during the trial

2. Not only is a leash not allowed, but your Sprocker Spaniel will not be allowed to wear a collar.

3. The handler is not allowed to touch your Sprocker Spaniel at any time during its run on the course.

4. You will be allowed to walk through the course before the competition starts. You will have to do your best to memorize the correct way to navigate the course, and will be given about 10 minutes to do so.

Keep in mind that there are always entry fees with agility trials and these are not generally refundable. The costs of competing can run up considerably if you have to travel long distances to get to the show: you will have lodging fees to contend with, as well as the normal costs associated with travel such as fuel costs. Keep in mind that if you have to rent a vehicle to attend a trial, that will also add to your total expenditure. Should you be traveling away from your home base, ask your veterinarian for a recommendation on a vet near where the trial will be taking place; it's better to know where to take your Sprocker Spaniel ahead of time should illness or injury occur.

There are certain basic things that you should bring with you to any agility trial: a crate for your Sprocker Spaniel with a pad or blanket for the bottom; a blanket to cover the crate to help keep it cooler; your Sprocker Spaniel's water dish, paper cups, and a supply of clean water; a chair for you to sit on; a hat; collar and leash. These should help to keep you and your Sprocker Spaniel comfortable during the competition. Do not neglect to bring along the means to clean up after your Sprocker Spaniel: a pooper scooper or appropriate bags.

You may also have to present your Sprocker Spaniel's vaccination record at the show, so be sure that you have a copy with you, your veterinarian should be happy to provide you with one. Even if a particular event does not require that you show proof of your Sprocker Spaniel's vaccinations, you should make certain that your Sprocker Spaniel is up to date on all of them – your Sprocker Spaniel will be around a lot of other dogs, so it's up to you to make sure that it has adequate protection. Because Kennel Cough spreads so easily, make sure that your Sprocker Spaniel has received this vaccination as well (this is an easy one, drops are simply put into your Sprocker Spaniel's nose).

Always remember that old maxim for travelers, "Take half the clothing you think you will need and twice the money." I have found myself that these are wise words and have served me very well when traveling, especially to a foreign country.

Speed Counts

Dogs are judged at an agility trial not only for their ability to navigate all the obstacles correctly, but also for the speed at which they do so. Adjustment is made with regards to the size of your Sprocker Spaniel, but regardless of the class, the fastest dog that completes the obstacle course correctly will be the winner. This is why it is important that you encourage your Sprocker Spaniel to take the obstacles as quickly as is safely possible.

Your Sprocker Spaniel will probably slow up a bit on your Dog Walk and Teeter-Totter, which is why it's a good idea to get your Sprocker Spaniel to move as quickly as they can on jumps, tunnel, and chute. During a trial you will understand the value of having taught your Sprocker Spaniel to go where you point and to listen to your commands – your Sprocker Spaniel will inevitably run faster than you, and by keeping it on course verbally and by pointing, you can really cut seconds off your run, especially if your Sprocker Spaniel is somewhat slow on your Dog Walk or Teeter-Totter. There is also a time limit on the run that your Sprocker Spaniel must keep within.

How Trials and Meets Are Conducted

When you begin to participate in agility with your Sprocker Spaniel, you will probably begin with meets. These are qualifying contests that will help you and your Sprocker Spaniel progress to the more challenging and prestigious trials. Dog clubs, such as the American Kennel Club (AKC), sponsor these trials. There are now literally thousands of meets and trials every year in countries around the world, and for those living in the United States or United Kingdom, it should not be difficult to find a meet appropriate for you.

To begin with, most agility organizations provide divisions to make the competition fairer in relation to breed and experience. These designations are meant to make the trials open to more people and their dogs and encourage participation. Keep in mind that no dog younger than 1 year of age will be allowed in an agility trial; some trials bar dogs younger than 18 months.

1. Novice class is for beginners in agility and offers a shorter course. This trial must be completed successfully, and your Sprocker Spaniel must have received a Novice title in order to go on to the next category. The pace of the course will be more at a trot rather than at a run.

2. Intermediate (Open) agility is for dogs that have been certified for the Novice class. The course is longer and more challenging than it is for the novices. At this level, your Sprocker Spaniel and its handler are expected to run through the course. This course is also longer than that for novices.

3. Advanced (Master or Elite) agility class is open for dogs that have received their Intermediate title. Not only will there be a stricter time limit, but the handler must stay farther away from their dog and communicate with it mostly by using hand signals.

4. Veterans class is open to older dogs, and gives these dogs a chance to show just how well an older dog can function. Jumps or hurdles will probably be set at a lower height, and the time limitations will not be as strict. A shorter obstacle course can also be offered.

In order to put your Sprocker Spaniel into the proper classification, measurements are taken for height at their shoulders (the withers). This will not only have bearing on how high the jumps will be set, but also for the timing of the course. Some trials will disqualify dogs if they fail to complete the course within a certain period of time while others will simply grade your Sprocker Spaniel, and award a fault, if it is too slow.

Faults

Faults are, in effect, black marks against your Sprocker Spaniel during the trial. Different organizations can have different designation of faults, and while some trials will simply keep track of the faults, others will immediately disqualify your Sprocker Spaniel if it commits one. A trial where the faults are simply noted and go towards lowering your Sprocker Spaniel's overall performance score is called a 'qualifying run'. These can be helpful in letting you know where your Sprocker Spaniel's weaknesses may lie, rather than being kicked off the field immediately. If your Sprocker Spaniel completes the course without being faulted, it will be said to have had a 'clean run'. Disqualification is why it's so important to make sure that your Sprocker Spaniel has been well trained in every aspect of agility, because the rules are strict.

Although each agility club will have specific errors that will be considered faults, you can expect your Sprocker Spaniel to be faulted on any combination of the following:

1. A Missed Contact can mean that your Sprocker Spaniel has not done an obstacle at all, or it can mean that it has not completed the obstacle. For instance, if your Sprocker Spaniel refuses to complete the Teeter-Totter or runs through the Pause Table, these are considered to be Missed Contacts.

2. A Knocked Bar will also constitute a fault. This can occur when your Sprocker Spaniel doesn't jump high enough and knocks the bar or plank on any of the jumps off its support.

3. A Refusal comes about when your Sprocker Spaniel simply refuses to tackle the obstacle in any way; dogs that will not enter the Tunnel or back away from a Jump will be faulted, and often will be disqualified immediately.

4. A Time Fault occurs when your Sprocker Spaniel has taken longer than is allowed for the completion of the obstacle course.

5. If your Sprocker Spaniel goes Off Course, by either one of your errors, it will be faulted.

6. A Weave Pole Fault occurs when your Sprocker Spaniel enters the Weave Poles on the left side, misses poles, or back-weaves to try to correct its error.

7. A Flyoff fault means that your Sprocker Spaniel has sailed off your Dog Walk or other elevated obstacle.

8. A Handling fault occurs if you touch your Sprocker Spaniel during the trial. Whether this was deliberate or accidental makes no difference, it is still a fault.

9. Unsportsmanlike behavior on the part of your Sprocker Spaniel's owner is considered a fault. This can include not only arguing with the judges, but also yelling at or striking your Sprocker Spaniel if it doesn't perform as you would like. Arguments with other contestants will also be a fault.

10. Defecating or urinating on the course will usually get a dog disqualified.

11. A Run-Out fault means that your Sprocker Spaniel has run off the course entirely.

12. Training in the Ring encompasses exactly what it states – the owner is trying to instruct your Sprocker Spaniel during the trial, rather than simply accompanying your Sprocker Spaniel.

Depending on the rules in effect at any particular trial, all of the above faults can mean instant elimination from the trial, or simply a demarcation. Because defecating or urinating during the trial is almost always an elimination, make sure that your Sprocker Spaniel has had a chance to walk off its latest drink and meal, and it's also advisable not to feed your Sprocker Spaniel generously right before the trial begins; a full stomach and/or bladder, combined with excitement can lead to trouble and your Sprocker Spaniel's disqualification.

And you should never forget that the best-trained Sprocker Spaniel can sometimes just have a bad day. Dogs can become overexcited easily, especially around other dogs and when exposed to crowds, noise, and a multitude of people. If your Sprocker Spaniel does mess up an agility trial and is eliminated, just chalk it up to experience. There is absolutely no excuse for punishing a dog that has ruined up its run; in most cases your Sprocker Spaniel will be fine at the next trial. However, if your

Sprocker Spaniel seems off in anyway, check it carefully for even small injuries – an infected toenail can cause a dog to refuse obstacles or run off course.

Being eliminated from an agility trial is not the end of the world, be sure you put this into perspective. In fact, over handling by the owner, providing a windmill of hand and arm signals and a chorus of verbal commands could well be at the bottom of the problem as your Sprocker Spaniel may well have simply become confused by what you were trying to tell it.

Chapter Sixteen: The Risks of Agility

Injuries

While we are all familiar with sports injuries that humans suffer, dogs are also subject to the same kind of injuries, and there can be no denying that agility contributes in no small measure to this. In the United States alone, approximately 1,000,000 dogs compete in agility trials each year, so it's not surprising that there will be injuries incurred by some of the participants. Some of the injuries are mild, of course, but some are serious and can cause permanent damage to your Sprocker Spaniel. There is no reason to forego agility because of a fear of injuring your Sprocker Spaniel, but anyone who is starting to participate in this sport should be aware of the potential for harm.

1. Sprains and muscle strains were the most frequently observed injuries, along with bruising. Yes, your Sprocker Spaniel can get bruised, its hair simply hides the injury.

2. Nearly 1/3 of dogs who are in agility become injured, and this is not only at trials, the rate of injury for home-based agility exercises is identical to the statistics for matches and trials.

3. Most of the injuries involved the feet, shoulders, spine, and neck.

4. Normal veterinary care after an injury can help prevent repeat injuries. Owners who relied on 'alternative' care such as massage and acupuncture were more likely to see their dogs injured again.

5. Approximately half of the injuries healed up within a month's time, while the other half required 2 months or more for the injury to heal. A small percentage of injuries resulted in permanent disability.

6. Although they are the most popular breed for agility, Border Collies were also the most likely to get hurt.

7. Not surprisingly, inexperienced dogs trained by inexperienced owners had higher rates of injury than people and dogs with several years of agility experience.

8. Any dog at an agility trial is more likely to be hurt when navigating your Dog Walk, Teeter-Totter, A-Frame, and any of the jumps.

Because intensive agility is a relative newcomer in the dog world, research is still being done to determine how best to treat many of the injuries so that your Sprocker Spaniel can return to the field as quickly as possible, and also how to prevent injuries from occurring in the first place. It is now recommended that any dog taking part in agility trials undergo a complete veterinary examination every 6 months, regardless of age, and even if your Sprocker Spaniel appears to be in perfect health. Dogs that have recovered from an injury should not only be examined before their next trial, but also every 3 months since previous injuries make it more likely that another injury will occur. Being aware of some of the more common injuries and familiarity with their treatment can help your Sprocker Spaniel stay active in agility.

Warm-Up Exercises Before a Trial

In the same way that human athletes need to warm up before a competition, so do canine athletes. If you take the time to warm your Sprocker Spaniel up before it starts its trial, the chances are that not only will your Sprocker Spaniel be less likely to get injured, but it will also give you a much better performance. You should set aside about half an hour before your Sprocker Spaniel is scheduled to compete to giving it a warm-up. The first step in this will be a 15 minute walk. This will get your Sprocker Spaniel's blood moving and start supplying more oxygen to the muscles. As more blood (and oxygen) arrives into the muscles, they become warmer and better able to handle stress. The warmed muscle will be able to respond much more quickly and will have a higher level of elasticity.

Besides giving your Sprocker Spaniel a walk, you can also help it to warm up effectively by having it go through some of the basic obedience commands. Tell your Sprocker Spaniel to 'Sit' and then tell it 'Down'. Repeating this several times will help loosen up the joints. As with walking your Sprocker Spaniel, this helps to get the joints and muscles warmed up nicely.

Stretching is particularly important as regards the shoulders, neck, and back; many of the agility injuries happen in these places. No, you will not be able to tell your Sprocker Spaniel to stretch while it starts doing so - you will have to help your Sprocker Spaniel stretch. Take your Sprocker Spaniel's right front leg and gently stretch it out; hold it in that position for several seconds and then return it to normal. You should do this about 5 times on each side. The same can be done for the hind legs. Just remember to use a smooth, gentle motion and avoid jerking your Sprocker Spaniel's legs.

You should also help your Sprocker Spaniel stretch its neck. You can do this by gently pushing your Sprocker Spaniel's head to the side until it touches the shoulders (don't force this, if you feel any real resistance, desist immediately), but a better way is to use a treat to tempt your Sprocker Spaniel to move its head in the desired direction itself. Do this 5 times on either side, and alternating sides will be especially beneficial.

Besides increasing circulation and warming the muscles and joints, warm-up exercises also help both you and your Sprocker Spaniel to relax. A relaxed dog will be less likely not only to make mistakes, but will also be less likely to be injured.

Have Fun!

Agility should be all about having fun with your Sprocker Spaniel, and by conducting it in a relaxed manner will not only make it more enjoyable for both of you, but it will help prevent injuries from occurring in the first place. Competition is a big part of agility, but never lose sight of the other aspects of the sport: bonding more closely with your Sprocker Spaniel, meeting like-minded people, working towards a goal, and simply having fun.

While there will be some minor injuries that the owner will be able to address him - or herself, if the injury seems more serious, or you have any doubts, make sure to take your Sprocker Spaniel to the veterinarian as soon as possible. Keep in mind that even minor hurts can become serious if they are not treated in a timely manner.

Also remember that some injuries will take weeks or months to heal completely, and that some Sprocker Spaniels will never be able to compete again. The fact that your Sprocker Spaniel can be seriously hurt or will be unable to attend agility trials again are why it is so important to train it carefully and never push or force. Stay vigilant for any sign of injury, regardless of how slight it seems, and attend to it immediately. Never force a dog that is limping or seems to be in pain back onto the field.

Have fun and love your Sprocker Spaniel

www.ingramcontent.com/pod-product-compliance
Lightning Source LLC
Chambersburg PA
CBHW030452010526
44118CB00011B/897